P9-ELF-704

Coins

Questions and Answers

by Clifford Mishler

Revised, Updated and Edited
by the Staffs of
**Numismatic News, World Coin News
and Bank Note Reporter**

Based on an Original Manuscript by
Carl Allenbaugh

Fourth Edition
Revised and Corrected Printing

 Whitman Coin Products

WESTERN PUBLISHING COMPANY, INC.
RACINE, WISCONSIN 53404

9359:595

Feature Index

Introduction

This new, totally revised and greatly expanded edition of *Coins, Questions and Answers* is bigger and better than ever. Packed into it's 208 pages are detailed answers to 713 frequently asked questions representing a broad spectrum of coin collecting interests. Enhancing the textual presentations are 283 detailed photographic illustrations.

The questions and illustrations presented have been carefully selected to provide the primary audience — novice, beginning or occasional collectors — with a feel for the historical significance of coins and the heritage they represent. This booklet is far more than an elemental text, however, as many of the questions posed would puzzle all but the most knowledgeable numismatists.

An ultimate problem solver, this booklet is, of course, certainly not; no question and answer book of manageable size could legitimately claim to provide the reader with more than an introduction to the diverse facets of the hobby which it's sweep encompasses. In fact, even a thousand compilations equal in volume to that presented between these covers would fall far short of achieving such a challenging objective.

Anyone seeking to investigate the fascinating historical facets of the coin collecting hobby will find, however, that this book ably fulfills the objective to which it was addressed ... providing informative, detailed answers to the selected basic, but challenging and interesting subjects which have puzzled legions of collectors for decades ... supplemented with timely questions on contemporary collecting topics.

We feel confident that the questions and answers presented will be enlightening and enticing to the beginner, providing him scholarly guidance along some of the more popular coin collecting trails, and at the same time refreshing and instructive to any but the most advanced numismatic students.

We hope this booklet will provide each reader with a point of beginning ... the novice with the motivation to proceed ... the beginner with the desire to progress ... the occasional collector with the determination to advance ... and the advanced collector with a sense of greater appreciation for the diversity encompassed in the realm.

So, read on colleague, to learn *what you should know ... but may have never asked!*

General Information

What is meant by the terms numismatics and numismatist?

Numismatics is the study and/or collecting of coins, paper money, tokens, medals, orders and decorations, and similar objects. A numismatist is one who has a comprehensive knowledge of numismatics. A collector isn't necessarily (indeed, seldom is) a numismatist: a numismatist needn't be a collector. He can be an archaeology associate, the curator of a national or institutional collection, a dealer, or simply a serious student of numismatics.

In various publications having to do with coin collecting I have noted a number of abbreviations which are very confusing to me. Could you explain the meaning of the ones most frequently encountered?

AE	— Bronze
AG or AU	— Gold
Al.	— Aluminum
ANA	— American Numismatic Association
ANACS	— ANA Certification Service
AR	— Silver
Ars.	— Arrows (at date)
Avg.	— Average
Bil.	— Billon
Br.	— Brass
Ca.	— About
Cmkd.	— Countermarked
C-N or Cop-Nic	— Copper-Nickel
Comm.	— Commemorative coin
Cu.	— Copper
Diad.	— Diademed

Drap.	— Drapery
Ind. Hd.	— Indian Head
IND:IMP	— Emperor of India
KL-numeral	— A catalog number from the book *Standard Catalog of United States Paper Money*
KM-numeral	— A catalog number from the book *Standard Catalog of World Coins*
1864-L	— An Indian Head cent with "L" on headress ribbon
Laur.	— Laureate
LD	— Large Date
3-Leg.	— A 3-legged major-error variety of 1937-D nickel
Let. Ed.	— Lettered Edge
Lg.	— Large
Lib.	— Liberty
LL	— Large Letters
Micro	— Smaller than usual mint mark
mm	— Millimeters (coin diameter)
MM or mmk.	— Mint Mark
N.C.	— No Cents
N.D.	— No date
Ni.	— Nickel
NM	— None Minted
Obv.	— Obverse
P-numeral	— A catalog number from the book *Standard Catalog of World Paper Money*
Pb.	— Lead
Pl.	— Plain
Pl. Ed.	— Plain Edge
Pt.	— Platinum
R-numeral (as R-1)	— Indicates degree of rarity
Rev.	— Reverse
SD	— Small Date
SL	— Small Letters
Sm.	— Small
Sn.	— Tin
Std.	— Seated
Stg.	— Standing
T or Ty.	— Type
Var.	— Variety
V.D.B.	— Victor D. Brenner (coin designer)
W.C.	— With Cents
w/o	— Without
Wtd.	— Wanted
Z	— Zinc
42/41	— Overdate

*	— An asterisk in a catalog indicates that the described coin is illustrated
Y-numeral	— A catalog number from the book *Modern World Coins* or *Current Coins of the World*

STANDARD COIN CONDITION ABBREVIATIONS & DEFINITIONS

P.	— Poor: Less desirable than FAIR, yet identifying features can usually be distinguished.
FR.	— Fair: Quite badly worn and highly undesirable, except for the rarest issues.
A.G.	— About Good
G.	— Good: Worn but lettering and design all clear.
V.G.	— Very Good: Definite signs of wear but not altogether unattractive.
A.F.	— About Fine
F	— Fine: Perceptible signs of wear but still a very desirable piece.
V.F.	— Very Fine: Showing inconsequential signs of wear.
E.F., EX.F. or XF	— Extremely Fine: No definite signs of wear, but having a less desirable surface than an uncirculated coin.
A.U.	— Almost Uncirculated.
MS	— Mint State; Followed by numeric designations from 60 through 70, representing varying degrees of quality from basic uncirculated to perfect quality as originally minted.
UNC.	— No signs of wear other than possible bag marks, but not necessarily brilliant. Used interchangeably with MS-60.
B.U.	— Brilliant Uncirculated. Sharply struck with full mint luster. May exhibit toning. Used interchangeably with MS-65.
GEM	— An uncirculated coin of nearly perfect quality.
PR.	— Proof: A piece produced by a technique involving specially prepared dies and planchets and usually special striking.
CR. UNC. or CU	— Crisp Uncirculated: Paper money which has not been in circulation.

UNC.	EX.F	V.F.	F

I have often heard people refer to the grade of a coin. What do they mean?

They are referring to the relative condition, or state of preservation of the coin in question. Grading a coin is basically a subjective exercise, but there are three grading "standards" that have been stated in textbook form and are widely referenced by dealers and collectors when they are judging the relative merits of a grading determination.

Each of these standard grading references possess unique distinctions. The first published (1958), and least referenced today, is Brown and Dunn's "A Guide to the Grading of United States Coins;" it is based on textual descriptions accompanied by line drawing illustrations of the various coinage types which are individually highlighted by grade to emphasize the degree of wear allowable for each condition level. Another title, James F. Ruddy's "Photograde," was published a decade later (1970); it presents textual descriptions representing similar characteristics of quality for each grade, accompanied by illustrative art in the form of reproductions of actual coin photos.

In 1977 the American Numismatic Association published the "Official A.N.A. Grading Standards for United States Coins." Where the previous titles presented grading descriptions which represented the opinions of the individual authors, the new title was a committee effort that represented the consensus of many individuals. It also introduced to general use in the grading of U.S. coins a numerical system intended to enhance and provide uniformity in the application of grading standards, the adjectival standards having been subjected to many variations of description and interpretation.

When a coin is described as being of MS-65 quality, what does that designation mean?

It is a numerical description of a quality which would be adjectivally described as being "choice uncirculated." It is one of a number of numeric designations on a scale from 3 to 70 used to designate coin grades, the lower number representing the lowest identifiable quality, 70 the highest. Numeric designators below 60 are accompanied by abbreviations of their adjectival counterparts; those from 60 through 70 by the letters MS, for "Mint State." In declining order of quality, the officially described designators and their adjectival counterparts are:

MS-70 Perfect Uncirculated	EF-45 Choice Extremely Fine
MS-67 Gem Uncirculated	EF-40 Extremely Fine
MS-65 Choice Uncirculated	VF-30 Choice Very Fine
MS-63 Select Uncirculated	VF-20 Very Fine
MS-60 Uncirculated	F-12 Fine
AU-55 Choice About Unc.	VG-8 Very Good
AU-50 About Uncirculated	G-4 Good
	AG-3 About Good

Individuals frequently describe coins by applying unofficial variations of these designators, like "Gem MS-65," MS-65+ and MS-64. Such indications are generally intended to enhance the reception of a coin which is clearly superior in quality to that represented by the next lower designator, although it will not meet the requirements of the next higher designator.

What do the abbreviations like ANA, NLG and FUN that I see some people list following their names, and dealers in conjunction with their business names?

Such letter combinations would generally represent abbreviations for national, regional, state and major specialized organizations, lists of which follow:

NATIONAL ORGANIZATIONS

American Numismatic Association (ANA) — Membership Department, American Numismatic Association, 818 N. Cascade Ave., Colorado Springs, CO 80903-3279. Annual dues: regular $21, junior (11-17) $11, associate $4; additional $5 application fee, first year only. Publishes: The Numismatist, a monthly magazine. Objectives and services: A non-profit educational organization dedicated to advancing the knowledge of numismatics and facilitating better cooperation and closer relations between numismatists. Maintains a museum and loaning library, sponsors national conventions semi-annually, sponsors young numismatist and educational programs, offers a grading and authentication service, plus photographic services and a numismatic insurance plan.

American Numismatic Society (ANS) — Leslie A. Elam, American Numismatic Society, Broadway at 155th St., New York, NY 10032. Annual dues: associate membership $20. Publishes: ANS Newsletter, a quarterly activities report; ANS Museum Notes, an annual journal; and Numismatic Literature, a semi-annual bibliography of studies published throughout the world. Objectives and services: Dedicated to the advancement of numismatic knowledge, the ANS was founded in 1858. It sponsors and publishes technical reference works that are offered to members at special prices. It maintains a comprehensive museum of U.S. and worldwide numismatic issues, along with a voluminous research library, presents annual graduate student seminars each summer, and a fall conference on Western Hemisphere Coinage topics.

Canadian Numismatic Association (CNA) — Executive Secretary, Canadian Numismatic Association, P.O. Box 226, Barrie, Ont. L4M 4T2, Canada. Annual dues: regular $20, junior $10. Publishes: The Canadian Numismatic Journal, a monthly scholarly journal published 11 times a year. Objectives and services: The encouragement and promotion of the science of numismatics with special emphasis on materials pertaining to Canada. Maintains a lending library for the use of members and sponsors an annual summer convention hosted at different sites each summer.

Numismatic Literary Guild (NLG) — David Thomason Alexander, Exectuive Director, P.O. Box 970218, Miami, FL 33197. Annual dues: regular $10. Publishes: NLG Newsletter, an every other month publication of topical interest. Objectives and services: To provide a forum for exchanges of ideas and interests among writers on numismatic subjects.

Professional Numismatists Guild (PNG) — Paul L. Koppenhaver, Executive Director, P.O. Box 430, Van Nuys, CA 91408. An organization comprised of approximately 200 leading rare coin firms, companies and individuals who are required to meet strict financial and professional requirements, including adherence to a strict Code of Ethics which provides for binding arbitration in the event of a disagreement between a member dealer and a customer.

Sociedad Numismatica de Mexico (SNM) — Board of Directors, Sociedad Numismatica de Mexico, Eugenia 13-301, Mexico 18, D.F., Mexico. Annual dues: regular $12 (U.S. funds); initiation fee $5. Publishes: Boletin, a quarterly journal. Objectives and services: Holds monthly meetings in Mexico City, and sponsors an annual convention.

SPECIALIZED ORGANIZATIONS

Active Token Collectors Organization (ATCO) — Bill Clapper, Editor, P.O. Box 1573, Sioux Falls, SD 57101. Annual dues: regular $15. Publishes: ATCO, a monthly trader journal published 11 times a year. Objectives and services: To increase collector knowledge of tokens by offering the best trading publication available to token and medal collectors.

American Tax Token Society (ATTS) — Tim Davenport, Secretary, P.O. Box 614, Corvallis, OR 97339. Annual dues: regular $5. Publishes: ATTS Newsletter, a quarterly of news and information for members. Objectives and services: Provide a research incentive and communications vehicle to promote the study and collecting of tax tokens and related subjects.

American Vecturist Association (AVA) — Donald Mazeau, Secretary, 46 Fenwood Dr., Old Saybrook, CT 06475. Annual dues: regular $12; plus $1 initiation fee the first year. Publishes: The Fare Box, a monthly report of new issues and discoveries. Objectives and services: A "vecturist" is a person dedicated to the study and/or collection of transportation tokens, the AVA being dedicated to assisting those who share an interest in the issue.

Bank Token Society (BTS) — John D. Mullen, Secretary-Treasurer, P.O. Box 383, Newtonville, MA 02160. Annual dues: regular $3; junior $1.50. Publishes: The Bank Examiner, a quarterly newsletter. Objectives and services: To identify, study and record information related to bank exonumia. Offers the availability of a lending library and free newsletter classified ads for members.

Canadian Paper Money Society (CPMS) — Dick Dunn, Secretary-Treasurer, P.O. Box 465, West Hill, Ont. M1E 2P0, Canada. Annual dues: regular $20. Publishes: The Canadian Paper Money Journal, a scholarly quarterly journal. Objectives and benefits: Encourage and support historical studies of banks and other note-issuing authorities in Canada, and preserving historical records relating thereto. Developing a reference library and statistical records archive to ensure that a record of Canada's early economic development is preserved.

Check Collector's Round Table (CCRT) — Charles Kemp, Secretary, 2075 Nicholas Ct., Warren, MI 48092. Annual dues: regular $10. Publishes: The Check List, a quarterly newsletter. Objectives and benefits: For individuals interested in the collecting, preservation and research of old and new bank checks, drafts, money orders, deposit receipts, notes, autographs, stock and bond certificates, engravings, vignettes and protectographing methods.

Civil War Token Society (CWTS) — Cindy Grellman, Secretary, 6733 Post Oak Lane, Montgomery, AL 36117. Annual dues: regular $7. Publishes: The Copperhead Courier, a quarterly journal on Civil War token subjects. Objectives and services: Stimulate and maintain interest in the field of Civil War token collecting.

Combined Organizations of Numismatic Error Collectors of America (CONECA) — Mark Lighterman, 9230 S.W. 59th St., Miami, FL 33173. Annual dues: regular $14, junior (under 18) $6; First Class mailings add $5. Publishes: Errorscope, a monthly magazine featuring error information and club news. Objectives and services: An educational, non-profit club organized to further the knowledge, study and sharing of interests in numismatic errors and varieties. Annually sponsors an Errorama Convention dedicated to the promotion of these interests; maintains a lending library of pertinent references.

Dedicated Wooden Money Collectors (DWMC) — Mrs. Ruby Threlkeld, Secretary, 1028 Azales Ct., La Marque, TX 77568. Annual dues: regular $5. Publishes: Timber Times, a monthly newsletter published 11 times a year. Objectives and services: Promoting the collecting of wooden nickels and related issues, with a particular focus on official and semi-official issues.

Early American Coppers (EAC) — Rod Burress, Membership Chairman, 9743 Leacrest, Cincinnati, OH 45215. Annual dues: regular $16, 1st class publication mailing $23. Publishes: Penny-Wise, a six times per year loose-leaf journal style newsletter. Objectives and services: Serves as a point of contact and information interchange for collectors of U.S. large cents, half-cents, colonial and hard times tokens. Sponsors a lending library, regional meetings at several locations throughout the country during the year, and a national meeting hosted in a different city each year.

The Elongated Collectors (TEC) — Al Kirka, Secretary, 116 Oak St., Manchester, CT 06040. Annual dues: regular $5. Publishes: TEC News, a quarterly newsletter on elongated coin topics. Objectives and services: Provide an organization for the exchange of information on elongated coin collectibles.

International Association of Silver Bar Collectors (IASBC) — Judy Drugan, Secretary, P.O. Box 3184, Kent, OH 44240. Annual dues: collectors $15, dealers $25. Publishes: club bulletin issues quarterly. Objectives and services: To promote the collecting of art bars and silver rounds.

International Bank Note Society (IBNS) — Milan Alusic, Secretary, P.O. Box 1642, Racine, WI 53405. Annual dues: regular $17.50. Publishes: IBNS Journal, a scholarly journal that appears on a quarterly basis; Inside IBNS, an occasional newsletter of society and general information especially for the membership that appears approximately quarterly. Objectives and services: Dedicated to fostering bank note collecting on a worldwide basis by promoting, stimulating and advancing the study and knowledge of issues, through the publication of information and studies on specialized interest areas.

International Organization of Wooden Money Collectors (IOWMC) — N.R. Mack, P.O. Box 395, Goose Creek, SC 29445. Annual dues: regular $5; after July 1, $2.50 for balance of year. Publishes: Bunyan's Chips, a monthly newsletter published 11 times a year. Objectives and services: Promote fellowship, freindship and knowledge among collectors interested in wooden money and related issues.

National Scrip Collectors Association (NSCA) — Walter Caldwell, Secretary, P.O. Box 29, Fayetteville, WV 25840. Annual dues: regular $10. Publishes: Scrip Talk, a 4-6 issue per year newsletter. Objectives and services: Dedicated to collecting, studying, researching and promoting metal and paper coal company scrip, lumber tokens, and related mining and manufacturing issues.

Numismatics International (NI) — Ross Schraeder, Secretary, P.O. Box 836094, Richardson, TX 75083. Annual dues: regular $15, junior (under 18) $10, senior (70 or older) $10. Publishes: NI Bulletin, a monthly journal of information. Objectives and services: Promote the science of numismatics by encouraging the sale, trade, discussion and display of coins and currency of all countries outside the U.S. Offers members use of a lending library and attribution service; is building a reference collection, and publishes original reference works and selected reprints.

Oriental Numismatic Society (ONS) — William B. Warden, Jr., Secretary — American Region, P.O. Box 356, New Hope, PA 18938. Anual dues: regular $10, first year $11. Publishes: ONS Newsletter, six issue per year membership and scholarship newsletter; Numismatic Ramblings, a general information newsletter for the American Region, published six times a year; Information Sheet and Occasional Paper, technical studies released sporadically. Objectives and services: Promote the systematic study of coins, medals and currency, both ancient and modern, of India, and Far East, the Islamic countries and their non-Western predecessors.

Society of Paper Money Collectors (SPMC) — Ronald Horstman, New Member Coordinator, P.O. Box 6011, St. Louis, MO 63139. Annual dues: regular and junior $20. Publishes: Paper Money, a bimonthly journal published in odd months. Objectives and servives: Encourage the collecting and study of paper money, with concentration on the colonial; obsolete, Confederate, National Currency and general issue notes of the U.S. government. Has sponsored the publication of several pioneering reference books on the obsolete currency issues of individual states.

Society of Philatelists and Numismatists (SPAN) — Joe Ramos, 1929 Millis St., Montebello, CA 90640. Annual dues: regular $5. Publishes: ExSPANsion, a newsletter, six issues annually, presenting information on the philatelic-numismatic combinations (PNC) hobby. Objectives and services: Promotion of the educational aspects of the PNC hobby.

Society of Ration Token Collectors (SRTC) — Robert A. Johnson, Secretary, P.O. Box J, Baltimore, MD 21228. Annual dues: regular $5. Publishes: The Ration Board, a quarterly newsletter of scholastic content. Objectives and services: Dedicated to research efforts on ration tokens and related issues.

Souvenir Card Collectors Society (SCCS) - Dana Marr, Secretary, P.O. Box 4155, Tulsa, OK 74159. Annual dues: collector $15, dealer $20. Publishes: Souvenir Card Journal, a quarterly publication presenting souvenir card and membership news and information. Objectives and services: Provides a centralized source of information on the variety of postal and currency vignette souvenir cards prepared by security printing firms, including the maintaining of a standard numbering system to record issues.

Token and Medal Society (TAMS) — Dorothy Baber, Secretary, 611 Oakwood Way, El Cajon, CA 92021. Annual dues: regular (incl. Canada and Mexico) $10, overseas $15. Publishes: TAMS Journal, a scholarly journal published six times annually. Objectives and services: Promote, stimulate and disperse knowledge on the history of collecting of tokens and medals. Members may borrow references from a substantial lending library. The society sponsors the publication of original reference works and reprints of out-of-print standards, and provides numerous award programs to encourage orignal research and cataloging.

Society for United States Commemorative Coins (SUSCC) — Jay Mercer, Secretary, 151 Elm St., New Cannan, CT 06840. Annual dues: regular $15, junior $5. Publishes: The Commemorative Trail, a quarterly journal of news and information on new discoveries and information in the commemorative collecting field. Objectives and services: Stimulate interest in collecting all U.S. commemorative issues. Hosts an annual meeting in conjunction with the ANA convention.

REGIONAL ORGANIZATIONS

Blue Ridge Numismatic Association (BRNA) — Shirley Townsend, Secretary, 409 O'Neal Dr., Birmingham, AL 35226. Annual dues: regular $5, junior $2. Publishes:

BRNA Journal, a quarterly news and membership information journal. Objectives and services: Dedicated to perpetuating numismatic interests throughout a string of southern states east of the Mississippi, stretching from Mississippi through North Carolina.

Central States Numismatic Society (CSNS) — Robert Douglas, Secretary, P.O. Box 223, Hiawatha, IA 52233. Annual dues: regular $3, junior (11-18) $1. Publishes: The Centinel, a quarterly magazine. Objectives and services: To promote numismatics and educate the public on coin collecting topics throughout a 13 state area stretching from Ohio and Kentucky to the east to North Dakota and Kansas in the west. Meets annually in convention during the spring in a major city within the Central States region, and also maintains a speakers bureau to provide programs to coin clubs and other interested organizations within the area.

Colorado-Wyoming Numismatic Association (CWNA) — L. Hellene Bohler, Secretary-Treasurer, 519 West Mountain, Fort Collins, CO 80522. Annual dues: $3.50. Publishes: CWNA Quarterly, presenting news of the association in conjunction with informative articles on numismatic subjects. Objectives and services: Promotion of interest in numismatics in the two-state area.

Great Eastern Numismatic Association (GENA) — Joseph Ridder, 30 Fairview Ave., Nanuet, NY 10954. Annual dues: regular $5, junior $2. Objectives and services: Promote coin collecting in the eastern region in and around the population belt running from New York City to Philadelphia. Meets annually in convention during the early fall.

Middle Atlantic Numismatic Association (MANA) — MANA Headquarters, P.O. Box 6266, Washington, DC 20015. Annual dues: regular $5, junior $3. Publishes: MANA Journal, a quarterly digest of numismatic and membership information. Objectives and services: To bring the numismatists of the Middle Atlantic area into closer relationship with one another for mutual improvement through the interchange of ideas and discussions, especially at annual conventions hosted in major cities in the Middle Atlantic area stretching from New York state in the north to North Carolina in the south.

New England Numismatic Association (NENA) — Eliott L. Goldberg, Executive Secretary, P.O. Box 99, West Roxbury, MA 02132. Annual dues: regular $5, junior $2.50. Publishes: NENA News, a quarterly journal of association news. Objectives and services: To serve the interests of numismatics throughout the six state New England region. Convenes at an annual fall convention.

Northern California Numismatic Association (NCNA) — Edward Sins, Treasurer, P.O. Box 5075, San Jose, CA 95150. Annual dues: regular $2. Publishes: NCNA Heads and Tales, a quarterly newsletter of member and club information. Objectives and services: To promote and serve numismatic interests in northern California; annually sponsors a convention in San Francisco during September.

Numismatic Association of Southern California (NASC) — Richard Lebold, Corresponding Secretary, Box 5173, Buena Park, CA 90622. Annual dues: regular $7. Publishes: The N.A.S.C. Quarterly, a journal presenting membership and scholastic content. Objectives and services: To promote and serve numismatic interests in southern California; annually sponsors a convention in February at the Los Angeles Airport Hyatt Hotel.

Pacific Northwest Numismatic Association (PNNA) — Nina Nystrom, Membership Chairman, P.O. Box 17183, Seattle, WA 98107. Annual dues: regular $5, junior (18 and under) $2.50. Publishes: The Nor'Wester, a quarterly newsletter. Objectives and services: A non-profit organization that ties together the clubs and individual collectors of the three-state Pacific Northwest, plus the Canadian provinces of Alberta and British Columbia. Hosts annual conventions during the spring.

Penn-Ohio Coin Clubs (P-O) — By Place, Secretary-Treasurer, 612 White St., Toledo, OH 43605. Annual dues: regular $5. Publishes: The Penn-Ohio Journal, a quarterly publication presenting feature articles and news of club activities in the region. Objectives and services. To advance the knowledge and appreciation of coin collecting throughout the Ohio and western Pennsylvania region.

STATE ORGANIZATIONS

Alabama Numismatic Society (ANS) — Purnie Moore, Secretary, P.O. Box 3601, West End, Birmingham, AL 35211. Annual dues: regular $5, junior (11-17) $1. Publishes; Alabama News Letter, three or four issues per year. Objectives and services: To promote numismatic education through the presentation of exhibits and programs. Sponsors an annual convention in Birmingham every July.

Arkansas Numismatic Society (ANS) — Louis Dudderar, President, 115 Donaghey Bldg., Little Rock, AR 72201. Annual dues: regular $3, junior (11-18) $1. Publishes: Arkoin News, a quarterly membership journal. Objectives and services: Dedicated to the education and welfare of scholars and collectors of coins and other numismatic material who reside in the state. Meets semi-annually, including at a state convention held in July.

California State Numismatic Association (CSNA) — Ethel Lenhert, Secretary, P.O. Box 63, Upland, CA 91785. Annual dues: regular $10. Publishes: Calcoin News, a top ranked numismatic quarterly featuring scholarly articles, personality features, association news and member club activities. Objectives and services: Annually sponsors a free all-day international public numismatic educational symposium featuring leading authorities in the field, plus semi-annual conventions featuring educational forums, exhibits, bourse and special events, the spring show in northern California, the fall in the southern part of the state. An extensive lending library is available to members, assistance services including audio/visual programs are available to member clubs, and a California collection is maintained at the Old San Francisco Mint for public appreciation.

Florida United Numismatists (FUN) — Maude Brown, P.O. Box 2256, Clearwater, FL 33517. Annual dues: regular $5, junior $2. Publishes: FUN Topics, a quarterly journal of numismatic information and organizational news. Objectives and services: Advancement of numismatic education throughout the state. Annually sponsors the first big show of the year on the numismatic circuit.

Georgia Numismatic Association (GNA) — Michael W. Griffith, Secretary, P.O. Box 611, Lilburn, GA 30247. Annual dues: regular $5, junior $2.50. Publishes: GNA Journal, a newsy association publication that appears six times annually. Objectives and services: Coordination of numismatic promotional efforts throughout the state, including between clubs. Meets annually in convention, and annually sponsors three junior scholarships to the ANA Summer Seminar.

Hawaii State Numismatic Association (HSNA) — Correspondence address: P.O. Box 477, Honolulu, HI 96809; memberships are automatically extended to members of the Honolulu Coin Club which may be addressed at: P.O. Box 6063, Honolulu, HI 96818. Annual dues: regular $4, initiation $1. Publishes: Nu Hou Dala Paa, the membership newsletter. Objectives and services: The HSNA operates as an adjunct of the Honolulu Coin Club, the only active organization in the state, presenting a convention in the city each November.

Illinois Numismatic Association (IllNA) — Mark Wieclaw, Treasurer, 175 W. Wood St., New Lenox, IL 60451. Annual dues: regular $4 first year, $3 thereafter. Publishes: Coin Digest, a quarterly publication. Objectives and services: To provide an annual convention and publication, awards and speakers for the benefit of the numismatists of Illinois.

Indiana State Numismatic Association (ISNA) — David Rasor, Corresponding Secretary, 3410 Vance, Fort Wayne, IN 46805. Annual dues: regular $5, junior (12-18) $2.50. Publishes: ISNA News, a quarterly journal. Objectives and services: To advance the knowledge of numismatics along educational, historical and scientific lines through the dissemination of trustworthy information, including duplicates of ANA slide programs which may be borrowed by members for Beta and VHS viewing in their homes, thereby promoting greater general interest in the field. Hosts annual convention every June in Indianapolis.

Iowa Numismatic Association (INA) — Phyllis Owen Pratt, Secretary, P.O. Box 65356, West Des Moines, IA 50265. Annual dues: regular $5, juniors (to 18) $2. Publishes: The Iowa Collector, a journal conveying information of state-wide interest to the membership. Objectives and services: organized in 1938, the INA is the oldest state-wide organization in existence. Meeting annually in convention every September, it seeks to foster the advancement of coin collecting interests at all levels.

Kansas Numismatic Association (KNA) — Polly Young, Secretary, P.O. Box 1282, Hutchison, KS 67504. Annual dues: regular $10. Publishes: KNA Newsletter, a quarterly informational journal for the membership. Objectives and services: To coordinate activities and promote coin collecting interest throughout the state. Sponsors a convention annually during the spring.

Kentucky State Numismatic Association (KSNA) — Bernard Allgeier, President, 1026 Samuel St., Louisville, KY 40204. Annual dues: regular $2. Publishes: newsletter sent to members just preceding and following annual convention. Objectives and services: To promote numismatic interests in Kentucky. Annually presents convention, which in recent years has always been hosted in Louisville.

Louisiana Numismatic Association (LNA) — Patricia J. Reno, Secretary/Treasurer, Box 1162, Gretna, LA 70053. Annual dues: regular $5, application fee $1. Publishes: no regular publication. Objectives and services: Development of numismatic interests in the state.

Maine Numismatic Association (MNA) — Cheryl Maisch, Secretary-Treasurer, P.O. Box 1328, Auburn, ME 04210. Annual dues: regular $2. Publishes: MNA Newsletter, issued on an intermittent basis through the year. Objectives and services: Sponsors winter, spring and fall shows in different cities within the state.

Maryland State Numismatic Association (MSNA) — William R. Ayres, Jr., Membership Chairman, Box 88, Fork, MD 21051. Annual dues: regular $4, junior $2. Publishes: The Maryland Numismatist, issued quarterly. Objectives and services: Works to further the study of numismatics through the sponsorship of seminars, books, educational programs, club programs and an annual convention hosted in early fall.

Michigan State Numismatic Society (MSNS) — Ann Bobrofsky, P.O. Box 1157, Battle Creek, MI 49016. Annal dues: regular $2, junior $1. Publishes: The Mich-Matist, a quarterly journal offering features and organizational information. Objectives and services: To promote and coordinate organized activities and numismatic interest in the state through services to individual members and clubs. Activities are oriented around a big Thanksgiving weekend show hosted annually in the Detroit area and a spring show hosted annually in an out-state city.

Minnesota Organization of Numismatists (MOON) — Jerry Swanson, President, P.O. Box 565, Rochester, MN 55903. Annual dues: regular $3. Publishes: MOON Views, a quarterly membership newsletter. Objectives and services: To promote interest in coin collecting. Sponsors an annual convention in the Minneapolis area every October.

Mississippi Numismatic Association (MNA) — Brenda Bain, Secretary-Treasurer, P.O. Box 925, New Albany, MS 38652. Annual dues: regular $5. Publishes: MNA Newsletter, a quarterly newsletter presenting information of interest to the membership. Objectives and services: Development of coin collecting interest throughout the state; annually sponsors a spring convention in a major city of the state.

Missouri Numismatic Society (MNS) — Robert Cochran, Secretary, P.O. Box 1085, Florissant, MO 63031. Annual dues: regular $5, initiation fee $1. Publishes: Missouri Journal of Numismatics, a yearly publication, plus a monthly bulletin that is mailed to members. Objectives and services: Based in St. Louis the MNS hosted monthly meetings featuring educational programs, and sponsors an annual Coin Festival every August. It offers members use of a large numismatic library.

New Hampshire Numismatic Association (NHNA) — Jim Rolston, Secretary-Treasurer, Box 37, Greenland, NH 03840. Annual dues: regular $1. Publishes: The Nonagon, a quarterly newsletter of membership information. Objectives and services: Meets annually in convention during March.

Garden State (New Jersey) Numismatic Association (GSNA) — G.S.N.A. Inc., P.O. Box 248, Brick, NJ 08723. Annual dues, regular $5, junior (9-18) $3. Publishes: New Jersey Numismatic Journal, an informative, human interest oriented quarterly journal. Objectives and services: Advance the knowledge of numismatics along educational, historical and scientific lines, and assist in the development of research on New Jersey numismatics. Hosts an annual convention in June, plus an annual summer picnic for members and their families.

Empire State (New York) Numismatic Association (ESNA) — Edmund Wlodarski, Secretary, 8026 Trina Circle West, Clay, NY 13041. Annual dues: regular $4. Publishes: Newsletter, four issues published annually. Objectives and services: Promoting coin shows and educational programs to foster interest in coins. Sponsors an annual state convention each fall, plus a mini-convention in July.

North Carolina Numismatic Association (NCNA) — Russell E. Southworth, Secretary, P.O. Box 20653, Greensboro, NC 27420-0653. Annual dues: regular $5, husband and wife joint membership $8, junior (under 18) $2. Publishes: NCNA Journal, a quarterly publication. Objectives and services: To bring together in fellowship individuals, clubs and kindred organizations interested in the numismatic science. Sponsors an annual convention in a major city of the state, in addition to promoting the formation of clubs throughout the state.

Oklahoma Numismatic Association (ONA) — Barbara Teasley, President, P.O. Box 760382, Oklahoma City, OK 73176. Annual dues, regular $7, junior $1. Publishes: Mint Luster, a bi-monthly membership journal of activities and interests. Objectives and services: To educate the public in the field of numismatics.

To Pennsylvania Association of Numismatists (PAN) — P.A.N., P.O. Box 144, Pittsburgh, PA 15230. Annual dues: regular $5, additional family members $3, junior $3. Publishes: The Clarion, a quarterly journal, plus a monthly membership newsletter. Objectives and services: To foster the development of state-wide collecting interests. Holds meetings state-wide in five organizational districts in conjunction with regularly scheduled shows in those areas, and also sponsors an annual show in the fall.

South Carolina Numismatic Association (SCNA) — SCNA Membership Chairman, P.O. Box 12163, Columbia, SC 29211. Annual dues: regular $7, junior $3. Publishes: SCanner, a quarterly journal on topics of state-wide collector interest. Objectives and services: Dedicated to the promotion and advancement of numismatics in all its dimensions. Sponsors an annual convention during the fall season.

South Dakota Coin and Stamp Association (SDCSA) — Ruth Casper, Secretary-Treasurer, 935 N. Lincoln, Madison, SD 57042. Annual dues: regular $5, junior (under 18) $1. Publishes: Newsletter, a quarterly intended to assist members in their collecting and study of numismatic interests. Objectives and services: Promotion of numismatics and philately throughout South Dakota, membership being open to all who have a sincere interest in any aspect of these parallel fields.

Tennessee State Numismatic Society (TSNS) — Ruth W. Armstrong, Secretary, 1501 Akins Dr., Chattanooga, TN 37411. Annual dues: regular $5, junior $2.50. Publishes: TennCoin News, a quarterly covering membership interests. Objectives and services: To promote, protect and extend numismatic activities throughout the state. Two of the principal vehicles for achieving this objective are spring and fall shows sponsored alternately in the eastern and western sections of the state.

Texas Numismatic Association (TNA) — Eleanor Kennedy, Secretary, 2901 Silverleaf Dr., Austin, TX 78757. Annual dues: regular $10, junior $3. Publishes: The TNA News. Objectives and services: Coordinate efforts to develop numismatic interests state-wide through the efforts of individuals and clubs. Sponsors an annual convention in a major city of the state.

The Utah Numismatic Society (UNS) — Utah Numismatic Society, P.O. Box 15054, Salt Lake City, UT 84115. Annual dues: regular $7, family $15, junior $3. Publishes: Mintmaster, a monthly newsletter. Objectives and services: To promote friendly hobby developing interests among collectors of the greater Salt Lake City area and throughout the state; holds monthly meetings and sponsors an annual fall convention in Salt Lake City.

The Virginia Numismatic Association (VNA) — Mavern Powell, Jr., Secretary-Treasurer, 15 Heather Lane, Newport News, VA 23606. Annual dues: regular $7. Publishes: The Virginia Numismatist, an interesting and informative little journal, six issues of which are published throughout the state by acting as the liaison between local clubs, colectors and dealers in promoting the educational pursuite of the hobby. Sponsors an annual convention each fall, and through the years has sponsored the publication of several standard references on Virginia numismatic topics.

Numismatists of Wisconsin (NOW) — Hank Thoele, Secretary-Membership, P.O. Box 12703, Green Bay, WI 54307. Annual dues: regular $3, junior $1 (11-17 years; membership is in Wisconsin Young Numismatists, an affiliate of NOW). Publishes: NOW News, a quarterly covering state organizational and historical topics. Objectives and services: To encourage and promote interest in numismatics, cultivating friendly relations between collectors and clubs, encouraging and assisting new collectors and clubs. Annually sponsors a late spring show in a major city of the state.

What books would you recommend for a collector's library?

There are thousands of books available, ranging from general references to comprehensive studies of specialized numismatic fields. The new collector should select general references as aids to classify his coins and to help him choose a specialty, if his interest so dictates. Some of the better known works are:

A Guide Book of United States Coins (the Red Book), R.S. Yeoman; *Standard Catalog of United States Paper Money,* Krause and Lemke; *Paper Money of the United States,* Friedberg; *Major Variety and Oddity Guide of United States Coins,* F.G. Spadone; *Standard Catalog of World Coins,* Krause and Mishler; *Coins of the World,* Craig; *Photograde* (guide to grading U.S. coins), Ruddy; *Official A.N.A. Grading Standards for United States Coins; Handbook of U.S. Coins* (the Blue Book), Yeoman; *Standard Catalog of World Paper Money,* Pick; *Canadian Coins, Tokens and Paper Money,* Charlton; *Official Guide to Mint Errors,* Herbert, and *Coins of Canada,* Haxby and Willey.

I am a novice collector, and would like for you to define for me some of the common numismatic terms in the collector's vocabulary.

ALTERED — Deliberately changed, usually with a view to increasing the face value or numismatic value of a coin or note.

ANCIENT COIN — Generally any coin issued before 500 A.D.

BILLON — A low-grade precious metal alloy used for some minor coin issues, consisting usually of a mixture of less than 50-percent silver and copper, and sometimes coated with a silver wash.

BULLION — Uncoined precious metal in the form of bars, plates, ingots, etc., or also a reference used to designate the precious metal content of a coin.

BUST — The head, including at least a portion of the collar bone.

CIVIL WAR TOKENS — Private issue pieces usually made to the approximate size of the current U.S. cents which circulated during the Civil War because of a scarcity of small change.

COIN — Usually a piece of metal marked with a device, issued by a governing authority and intended to be used as money.

COMMEMORATIVE — A piece issued to mark, honor or observe an event, place or person, or to preserve its memory.

COPPER COIN — A coin containing over 95% pure copper. Lower grade alloys are usually termed bronze or brass.

COPY — A reproduction or imitation of an original.

CROWN — A general term embracing most silver coins from about 20 to 30 grams in weight and from about 33 to 50 millimeters in size. The term now applies to nickel alloy coins of similar weight and size.

CURRENT — Coins and paper money still in circulation.

DEVICE — The principal element, such as a portrait, shield or heraldic emblem, of the design on the obverse or reverse of a coin, token or medal.

Descriptive identification of a coin

DIE — A hardened metal punch, the face of which carries an intalgio or incuse mirror-image of the device to be impressed on one side of a planchet.

DUPLICATE — A piece identical to another, except that it need not be in the identical state of preservation.

EDGE — That portion of a coin, generally plain or reeded, which displays the thickness between it's obverse and reverse.

ERROR — A coin, token, medal or paper money item evidencing a mistake made in its manufacture.

EXERGUE — The lower field of a coin, usually on the reverse.

EXONUMIST — A collector whose interests encompass numismatic items outside those issued for official government monetary purposes.

FACSIMILE — An exact copy or reproduction.

FIELD — The blank space on a coin not occupied by the design.

FORGERY — An unauthorized copy made with intent to deceive.

FRACTIONAL COIN — A coin, the face value of which is a fractional unit of the denominated currency, generally minted of silver.

HARD TIMES TOKEN — An unofficial large-cent size copper struck in a wide variety of types during 1833-1844, serving as de facto currency and bearing a politically inspired legend, or with advertising, as a store card.

INCUSE — A design or lettering recessed into the surrounding surface of a coin.

INTRINSIC — As applied to value, the net metallic value as distinguished from face value.

LEGAL TENDER — Currency explicitly determined by a government to be acceptable in the discharge of debts.

LEGEND — The inscription on a numismatic item.

LETTERED EDGE — A design characteristic of coins whereby a piece when viewed by the edge will reveal a statement of the coin's denomination or a patriotic legend. On U.S. coins, lettered edges appear only on half-cents and large cents of 1792-95, halves and silver dollars minted prior to 1836, and on the Saint-Gaudens eagle and double eagle issues; the lettering appearing incuse on the early issues, raised on the eagles and double eagles.

MEDAL — Usually a piece of metal, marked with a design or inscription, made to honor a person, place or event.

MEDIEVAL COIN — A coin struck from about 500 to 1500 A.D.

MILLED COIN — By contrast with a hammered coin, a piece produced by pressure indirectly rather than directly applied, and the edge of which has been rolled or up-set.

MINOR COIN — A silver coin of less than crown weight or any coin struck in base metal.

MINT LUSTER — The sheen or "bloom" on the surface of an uncirculated numismatic item. Once removed, mint luster can never be restored.

MINT MARK — A letter or other symbol, sometimes of a privy nature, indicating the mint of origin.

MINT SET — One coin of each denomination produced by a given mint in a given year without regard to condition. Mint sets purchased directly from a mint contain uncirculated coins.

MISPRINT — An error in printing.

MODERN COIN — A coin struck after about 1500 A.D.

MONEY — A medium of exchange.

MULE — A coin made by using the dies of two different coins.

NCLT — An abbreviation designating official government issue "Non-Circulating, Legal Tender" coins, generally struck of silver or gold in denominations not intended to circulate commercially.

OBVERSE — The side of a numismatic item which bears the principal device. With a few exceptions, the obverse is the date side of regular-issue U.S. coinage.

PATINA — A natural surface coloring, induced by oxidation, acquired by all unprotected coins with the passage of time. Usually applied to the green film formed naturally on copper and bronze. Patina can also be produced artificially, as by acids.

PLAIN EDGE — A design characteristic of all U.S. small cents and nickels, half-cents and large cents minted after 1795, two-cents and three-cents pieces, and the silver 20-cents coin.

PLANCHET — The disc of metal or other material on which the dies of a coin, token or medal are impressed.

PROOF SET — A set of one proof coin of each current denomination issued by a recognized mint for a specific year.

REEDED EDGE — The design characteristic present on most U.S. silver and gold coin issues, and their successor clad metal coinages, consisting of a continuous encirclement of raised vertical lines.

REISSUE — A numismatic item issued again after an extended lapse of time.

RESTRIKE — A numismatic item produced from original dies at a later date.

REVERSE — The side of a numismatic item opposite to that on which the principal device is impressed.

RIGHT & LEFT — The viewer's right and left.

SCRIP — Paper currency, usually of denominations less than one dollar, issued as substitutes for currency by private persons or organizations.

SILVER COIN — A coin consisting of more than 50% silver content.

SPECIMEN — A coin or bank note prepared as an example of a given issue.

SPURIOUS — A false piece made to deceive, often an original creation rather than a copy of a known item.

STORE CARD — A token bearing a business name and/or address, and often intended as a local or ad-hoc medium of exchange.

TOKEN — Usually a piece of durable material and unofficially issued for monetary, advertising, services or other purposes.

TOKEN COINAGE — Coinage the intrinsic value of which is less than its face value.

TYPE SET — A collection composed of one coin of each basic design within a given range of issues.

UNIFACE — Showing a design on one side only.

UNIQUE — Existing in only one known specimen.

VECTURES — Transportation tokens.

A friend of mine has an 1877 Indian Head cent for which he had been offered several hundred dollars. I have an older 1871 half dime for which I have been offered only a few dollars. My coin is older, shouldn't it be worth more?

The age of a coin is not of itself significant in determining a coin's value. Coins of the ancient Greeks and Romans, or Medieval kings and Crusaders, can also be purchased for nominal amounts.

The value of a coin, as with any commodity, is determined by the interaction of supply and demand. Demand, as it applies to a specific coin, is determined by the popularity of the series, and the availability and condition of the coin.

Your friend's 1877 Indian Head cent is one of the "key coins" of a series widely collected by date and mint mark. The half dimes are commonly collected by type only, which drastically reduces the demand on what is actually a smaller total supply.

What benefits does a collector derive from joining a local coin club or national organization?

Three principal benefits can be derived from active membership in a local coin club: the mental stimulation of associating with people of like interests; the opportunity to increase knowledge through the club's program of guest speakers, by conversation with advanced collectors, and by intelligent use of the club's library; and the opportunity to upgrade and add to your collection by trading or selling your duplicates, and by purchase, often below market, from fellow members. Membership in a national organization affords an expanded opportunity for learning through advanced articles in the organization's publication, and by access to a larger lending library.

What useful purpose is served by attending a national, or major convention?

Obviously, a national convention enlarges the opportunity for fellowship and to buy and sell numismatic items. However, the average collector also appreciates the opportunity to browse among the exhibits, to study displays in every field of the numismatic endeavor, to see the fabulous rarities — the aristocrats of Coindom — he could see nowhere else.

What is meant when a reference is made to the bourse area and bourse tables?

"Bourse" is a French noun meaning purse, bag; stock exchange; scholarship, fellowship. In practice it indicates a meeting of purse and produce, or the marketplace. In numismatics, the bourse is that area of a convention facility set aside for the purpose of dealers in numismatic items and supplies. The table space a dealer rents is called his bourse table.

What categories of "collectibles" are covered by the Hobby Protection Act?

The Hobby Protection Act of November 29, 1973, requires that reproductions and imitations of numismatic and political items be marked as copies. Numismatic items include coins, tokens, paper money and commemorative medals. Political items include political buttons, posters, literature, stickers and advertisements. The Act applies only to items manufactured after enactment of the Act, and does not apply to any reissue or restrike of any original numismatic item by the United States or any foreign government.

The motto IN GOD WE TRUST first appeared on a coin of the U.S. in 1864, during the Civil War. Is that the year it became the national motto?

Although the presence or absence of the motto on our coins has been a highly emotional issue since 1864, and despite the fact that the inclusion of the motto in coin design was made mandatory by the Act of July 11, 1955, IN GOD WE TRUST did not become the national motto of the United States until July 30, 1956, when it was so decreed by a Resolution of the 84th Congress and was approved by President Eisenhower.

When did the motto E PLURIBUS UNUM first appear on our coins? Is use of the motto required by law?

The first use of the motto E PLURIBUS UNUM ("one composed of many") on the coinage of the United States was on the 1795 Liberty Cap-Heraldic Eagle gold half eagle. Its use was not directed by law until the Act of February 12, 1873, required that the motto be inscribed on all coins bearing a representation of an eagle. Nevertheless, the motto did not appear on the 1875-1878 20-cent piece, which bore an eagle on reverse.

I have often wondered what the Secret Service expects me to do if I am handed a piece of paper currency I recognize to be counterfeit.

There are certain things you can do if it doesn't expose you to personal danger. Do not return the note to the one who gave it to you. Telephone the nearest police station and give the answering officer all of the pertinent information you have gathered. Write your name or initials and the date on the note in ink before surrendering it to the police or Secret Service.

Early American Coins

Is the Pine Tree Shilling a rare coin?

No, but it is a scarce coin and commands a premium determined by variety and condition.

The Pine Tree coinage — shilling, sixpence and threepence — was issued by Massachusetts Colony from 1667 to 1682, but all were dated 1652. The British Crown forbade the issuing of coinage by the colonies to prolong their dependence on England. The Crown's displeasure was made known in 1652 upon the appearance of the Massachusetts NE or New England shilling, and all subsequent related issues — including the Willow Tree issues of 1653-1660 and the Oak Tree issues of 1660-1667 — carried that date as the colony continued to defy the crown.

What were the "Elephant Tokens"?

Little is known of them. They are generally regarded as half-penny tokens, presumably struck in England as a promotional piece to stimulate interest in the American Colonies. Two types, both dated 1694, are associated with the colonies by reverse legend: GOD PRESERVE NEW ENGLAND and GOD PRESERVE CAROLINA AND THE LORD PROPRIETERS. A third type, of similar obverse, is undated, bears the legend GOD PRESERVE LONDON, and is presumed to have been issued during the Great Plague of 1665 which claimed 100,000 Londoners.

If Hibernia was the English name for Ireland, how do you account for the listing of such a coin in the category of American Colonial coins?

The Hibernia farthing and halfpenny pieces of 1722-24 were coined, under Royal patent, by William Wood for use in Ireland. However, their preparation became so involved in political scandal and graft that the Irish people refused to accept them. Wood's patent was revoked, and the coins were sent to the colonies, where they were well received.

Did any of the original thirteen states issue their own coins after the Declaration of Independence?

During the period when the loosely federated colonies were governed by the Articles of Confederation, and before our present Constitution was adopted, all of the colonies considered their own coinage, and many authorized the production of it.

States which authorized and issued a coinage include: New Hampshire, Vermont, Connecticut, Massachusetts and New Jersey. A New York coinage was issued by a consortium calling themselves a "Manufactory of hardware," but there is no record that the state authorized their operation.

I have been told that shortly after the American Revolution, England issued a number of coins honoring George Washington. Is this true?

It should be remembered that the American Revolution was not without considerable sympathy in England, even in Parliament.

A great number and variety of Washington pieces were struck during the period from 1783 to 1795, including a number of half-penny tokens of English origin. Many of the pieces of American origin are of one-cent value. Some of the strikes were intended as patterns for half dollars. Mainly they feature a bust of Washington, patriotic slogans, and an early employment of the eagle and shield with stars.

Are all of the Washington pieces complimentary to him?

One is tempted to suppose that all of the pieces were distasteful to Washington, who was opposed to having his portrait on coins; and that he felt particularly uncomplimented by those depicting him with the laureated head traditionally reserved for royalty. An extremely rare 1784 piece, presumed to be of American origin, is so maliciously executed that it is known as the "Ugly Head" of Washington and cannot be considered complimentary by any given to rational thought.

Has a foreign coin ever been legal tender in the United States?

The Spanish milled dollar valued at 8 reales (popularly known as the "pillar dollar" and "piece of eight") was legal tender in the United States until 1857. This renowned coin, the favorite trade coin of international commerce for more than three centuries, was the principal coin of the American colonies and the forerunner of the silver dollar of the United States.

The influence of its fractional parts (or "bits") is still impressed upon our language. The 1 real coin, being an eighth of the Spanish dollar, had a value of 12½ ¢ U.S.; the 2 reales was valued at 25¢, etc. This is the origin of the slang expression "two bits" for a quarter.

I recently read a story concerning the cattle drives of the Old West in which the author casually employed the terms "dobe dollar" and "short bit". What did he have reference to?

The Texas drovers who pushed slab-sided longhorns up the Great Western and Chisholm trails to Dodge City and Abilene in those violent years following the Civil War had an acute suspicion of paper currency contracted from their experience with Confederate money. If they couldn't get U.S. cartwheels or California gold pieces, they took their pay in Mexican pesos, which they called 'dobe dollars. The 'dobe dollar circulated freely between the Mississippi and the Rockies long after foreign coin had been deprived of legal tender status.

Every mining camp and cowtown had its "bit house" which used the Spanish real or "bit" (valued at 12½ cents U.S.) as the unit of pricing. The "bit" could be a round Spanish 1-real coin, or it could be a pie-shaped piece made by cutting a piece of eight into quarters and then cutting the quarters in half to produce two normal or 12½ -cent bits. If the quarter was divided on a 60-40 basis, the larger piece, known as a "long bit," was valued at 15 cents and the smaller piece or "short bit" at 10 cents. The United States dime was also known as a "short bit."

What was the first coinage to be specifically struck for the English-American colonies, and when was it issued?

The first coinage for the English-American colonies was the "Hogge Money" of Bermuda which was coined in London, introduced into the colony between 1612 and 1616, and discontinued in 1624. "Hogge Money" was made of lightly silvered brass or copper, and was issued in denominations of twopence, threepence, sixpence and shilling. The name "Hogge Money" derives from the hog. The English found hogs in plentiful supply on Bermuda, the consequence of a Spanish shipwreck in the early 16th century.

What was the first coinage struck in America for the English-American colonies?

The Spaniards established a mint at Mexico City in 1535, and its real-denomination coinage eventually became the de facto currency of the English colonies in the New World. The first coins struck in North America for the English-American colonies were the silver threepence, sixpence and shilling which comprise the New England (NE) coinage struck between June 11 and October 19, 1652, at a mint just outside Boston. The issue was discontinued because its crude workmanship and simple design encouraged clipping and counterfeiting. It was superseded by the 1653-1660 Massachusetts Willow Tree coinage.

What was the first coin to be issued by authority of the United States, and when was it issued?

In the years following the American Revolution, commerce was plagued by a flood of underweight state coppers and forgeries of English issues. On April 21, 1787, Congress tried to ease the frustrating economic situation by ordering the striking of an official United States copper coin, known as the Fugio Cent. Congress directed that the coppers bear a representation of a sundial, the date 1787, FUGIO ("time flies") and the motto MIND YOUR BUSINESS on obverse; and thirteen linked circles and the motto WE ARE ONE on reverse. Because it is believed that Benjamin Franklin suggested the mottoes, these coppers are frequently called Franklin Cents.

The United States did not have a mint in 1787 and awarded a contract for the striking of 300 tons of Fugio coppers to a Mr. James Jarvis, part owner of a New Haven company that had coined coppers for the State of Connecticut. Jarvis defaulted on the contract, and produced but 400,000 Fugio coppers for the Treasury, most of which were struck early in 1788.

The Law of April 2, 1792, committed the United States to a decimal standard coinage, therefore isn't it true that the first official coins of the country bear a value expressed in terms of the decimal standard were the half disme and disme struck at the U.S. Mint in 1792?

Congress resolved as early as July 6, 1787, that the money unit of the United States "shall be one dollar," and that "the several pieces shall increase in a decimal ratio." In the years following the American Revolution, the Continental Congress permitted the states to coin money, with the Congress serving as a regulating authority. By that authority, Massachusetts struck cents in 1787 and half cents and cents in 1788 on which the value was expressed as "Half Cent" and "Cent." These are the first official coins to bear a stated value in terms of the decimal parts of the dollar unit in the country. The coins struck at the U.S. Mint in 1792 are considered to be patterns.

I have been told that the famous Brasher doubloon wasn't really a coin at all. Is this true?

Although the celebrated and historically significant Brasher doubloons are generally considered to be the first "gold coins" minted in the United States, it isn't positively known what they are, or were intended to be. Two theories have been advanced to account for their existence. Inasmuch as the doubloons were struck to the approximate diameter size of the cents then being issued by New Jersey, Vermont, Connecticut and Massachusetts, it has been proposed that the doubloon-size coins were actually pattern cents intended as samples for consideration by the New York State Assembly when Brasher

petitioned the Assembly for the right to coin coppers for New York State. It is, however, unlikely that Brasher would have placed his name so prominently on a die intended for an official copper coinage, or that he would have prepared a pattern in gold rather than copper. The other theory suggests that when his petition was rejected by the Assembly, Brasher added his name to the die and struck a number of specimens of doubloon weight and standard as mementos of his proposed cent, or to sell as curios in his souvenir shop.

There is no doubt that Brasher's doubloons could have served as a medium of exchange in the era of bullion coinage. They weighed about 408 grains, giving them an intrinsic value equal to that of the Spanish gold doubloon ($16).

Is it true that a coinage expressed in denominations of "marks", "quints" and "bits" was once considered for adoption by the United States?

On January 15, 1782, Robert Morris submitted a system of coinage devised by Gouverneur Morris, who had been Assistant Financier of the Confederation, which was designed to carry out the idea of a decimal system of coinage for the United States. The unit of the system was a quarter grain of fine silver. The coins were of silver, the lowest denomination, the "bit" or "cent," containing 25 grains of fine silver. The 500 unit designation was called the "quint," and the 1,000 unit designation a "mark." Patterns of the various denominations, known as the Nova Constellatio Patterns, were struck in silver for consideration by the Congress, but the coinage never advanced beyond the pattern stage. The patterns are all dated 1783 and are extremely rare.

The silver Nova Constellatio patterns shouldn't be confused with the Nova Constellatio coppers, which were struck in England in large quantities in 1783 and 1785 and imported into America by Gouverneur Morris as a private business venture.

I recently picked up a copy of a Colonial numismatic piece that has a picture of a deer on obverse and the legend VALUE ME AS YOU PLEASE. Can something so arbitrarily valued really have served as money?

Yes, usually at a value of threepence. These copper tokens were made by Dr. Samuel Higley, who owned a copper mine near Granby, Connecticut. He mined and smelted his own ore, engraved his own dies, and released the first issue of his Granby or Higley coppers in 1737. They bore a legend valuing the pieces at threepence. The number of pieces in circulation soon exceeded local demand, and people began to complain that the coppers were overvalued. With commendable imagination, Dr. Higley then created a new design on which his value of threepence was expressed by the Roman numeral III, but which in addition bore a legend inviting those who disagreed to value the tokens as they pleased.

Which of the states was the first to consider issuing its own coinage after the Declaration of Independence?

In 1776, the House of Representatives of New Hampshire authorized the limited production of an issue of copper coins. Patterns were prepared, but there is no evidence that they actually circulated, or were even approved.

What was the first silver dollar-size coin ever proposed for the United States?

That distinction belongs to the Continental Dollar of 1776, although it was probably struck only in pattern form and never reached general circulation. Specimens of this first U.S. dollar were struck in silver, pewter and brass. From their condition, it is likely that some of the silver coins actually circulated as dollars.

It is common knowledge that the English colonists in America obtained low-denomination silver coins by cutting the Spanish piece of eight into halves, fourths and eighths. Did they originate this practice?

From about 1180 (during the reign of Henry II) until Edward I (1272-1307) coined round silver half pennies and farthings, English silver pennies were made with a voided cross device on the reverse. This voided cross, which was essentially a cross with a center groove running the full length of each extension, enabled the penny to be easily and equally divided into halfpennies and "fourthings."

A number of the individual states issued their own coinage after independence from Great Britain was achieved. For how long did they have the right to do so?

The states had the right to coin money from July 2, 1776, the day independence from Britain was declared until ratification of the Constitution on June 21, 1788.

Is it true that the United States Congress once authorized the issuing of a "penny" (not a cent)?

On February 20, 1777, Congress proposed a half-ounce standard for an American "penny"; giving it a weight of 218.75 grains, which, interestingly, approximates the 224 grains, weight of brass specimens of the Continental dollar. It is possible that the Continental dollars, which bear no mark of value, were patterns for both a United States silver dollar and the only "penny" ever authorized by the United States government.

What is the difference between coins or tokens identified as Colonial issues, Early American issues and issues of the States of the Confederation?

Colonial pieces were issued before the American Revolution. Early American pieces were issued either during the Revolution or during the infancy of the United States. The coinage of the States of the Confederation consists of state-authorized issues which came into being between the Declaration of Independence and the ratification of the Constitution. Colonial and Early American issues may be, and usually are, of private origin.

Which was the first of the states to issue an official coinage after the Revolution?

Vermont is recognized as the first state to issue an official copper coinage although it did not have state status under the Articles of Confederation at the time. On June 15, 1785, the Vermont Assembly granted Reuben Harmon, Jr. the exclusive right to coin coppers for the state. The first Vermont coppers had a representation of the Green Mountains on obverse and the Eye of Providence on the reverse. In 1786 the obverse was given a design of laureated head and the reverse that of a seated woman, thus deliberately giving the coppers a distinct resemblance to the English halfpenny to facilitate their acceptance throughout the Confederation.

What was the metallic composition of the underweight "bath" metal Rosa Americana coinage of William Wood that the colonists refused to accept?

Bath metal is an alloy of 75 percent copper, 24.7 percent zinc and .3 percent silver.

Most of the tokens struck by or for England's colonists in America bear the "pence" denominations of the English coinage system. Spanish coins were the favored currency of the colonists. Weren't any tokens struck in denominations of the Spanish system?

The coins in shortest supply in the colonies were low-denomination copper issues. When present, they were usually English halfpennies, real or counterfeit. Richard Holt, an English tin producer, struck tokens for the English colonies in nearly pure tin, in Spanish style, and gave them a value of 1/24 real to facilitate their acceptance in America and the West Indies. The colonists regarded the tin Richard Holt Plantations Tokens as "leaden and pewter farthings" and refused to accept them.

United States Coins

General Information

What coins have been officially issued in the United States, and are they all still legal tender?

With a single exception (the 1873-1885 Trade dollar), all coins ever officially issued by the government remain legal tender to this day, as do all issues of paper money. Here is a list of the coins and their years of actual and official issue:

Half cent — 1793-1857
Large cent — 1793-1857
Small cent, copper-nickel — 1857-1864*
Small cent, bronze — 1864-1942, 1944-1982†
Small cent, zinc coated steel — 1943
Small cent, copper coated zinc — 1982-date
Two cent — 1864-1873
Three cent, .900 silver — 1851-1873
Three cent, nickel — 1865-1889
Half dime, .8924 silver — 1794-1837; .900 silver — 1837-1873
Five cent, nickel — 1866-1942, 1946-date
Five cent, silver alloy — 1942-1945
Dime, .8924 silver — 1796-1837; .900 silver — 1837-1964
Dime, clad/cupronickel — 1965-date
Twenty cent, .900 silver — 1875-1878
Quarter dollar, .8924 silver — 1796-1838; .900 silver — 1838-1964
Quarter dollar, clad/cupronickel — 1965-date
Quarter dollar, clad/40% silver — 1976§
Half dollar, .8924 silver — 1794-1836; .900 silver — 1836-1964, 1982 Washington Commemorative
Half dollar, clad/40% silver — 1965-1970; 1976§
Half dollar, clad/cupronickel — 1971-date

Dollar, .8924 silver — 1794-1803; .900 silver — 1840-1873, 1878-1935, 1983-
date, commemoratives§

Dollar, clad/40% silver — 1971-1976§

Dollar, clad/cupronickel — 1971-1978, 38.1mm diameter

Dollar, clad/cupronickel — 1979-1981. 26.5mm diameter, Susan B. Anthony

Trade dollar, .900 silver — 1873-1885‡

Gold dollar, .900 gold — 1849-1889

Quarter eagle ($2.50), .9167 gold — 1796-1834; .8992 gold — 1834-1839; .900
gold — 1840-1929

Three-dollar gold, .900 gold — 1854-1889

Half eagle ($5) .9167 gold — 1795-1834; .8992 gold — 1834-1838; .900 gold —
1839-1929, 1986 Statue of Liberty

Eagle ($10), .9167 gold — 1795-1804; .900 gold — 1838-1933, .900 gold —
1838-1933; 1984 Olympics§

Double eagle ($20) .900 gold — 1849-1933•

Fifty-dollar gold — a 1915 commemorative issue⋆

* There are small cents dated 1856 that are frequently included in date sets,
but they were not an authorized issue, and are regarded as patterns.

† Various metallic composition variations were employed in the manufacture
of bronze cents, ranging from a composition of 95% copper and 5% tin and
zinc (1864-1942) to 95% copper and 5% zinc (1962-1982).

§ Struck for sale to collectors, but legal tender.

‡ This dollar was intended for circulation outside the United States, primarily in the Orient, but was legal tender to the extent of $5 during the
period of 1873-1876.

• Although the $20-gold piece was struck in 1933, it is an uncollectible coin,
as none were officially released.

⋆ During the period of 1892-1954, the United States issued 60 major types of
commemorative coins, this being the only issue that was not produced in a
standard denomination and metal.

*What mints have operated at one time or another to strike United States
coins?*

CC — Carson City, Nev. (1870-1893)

 C — Charlotte, N.C. (gold coins only, 1838-1861)

 D — Dahlonega, Ga. (gold coins only, 1838-1861)

 D — Denver, Colo. (1906-date)

 O — New Orleans, La. (1838-1861, 1879-1909)

 P — Philadelphia, Pa. (1792-date)*

 S — San Francisco, Calif. (1854-1955, 1968-date)

 W — West Point, N.Y. (1984 Olympics Gold $10)

*No mint mark appears on Philadelphia Mint coins, except the five-cent
pieces of 1942-1945, the 1979-P Dollar and 1980 and subsequent dated issues,
excepting the cent.

*Are there any specific reasons why we do not change the design of our
coins as frequently as do foreign countries?*

A law enacted by Congress on September 26, 1890, establishes that changes in the design of regular-issue United States coins cannot be made more frequently than once every twenty-five years, except by an enabling Act of Congress.

Treasury officials maintain that the counterfeiting of our coins and currency is made more difficult by infrequent design change; reasoning that familiarity intimately acquaints the public with the designs, enabling them to more readily detect counterfeits. If you believe this reasoning to be valid, ask a noncollector to describe the reverse of the coins in his pocket.

What are proof coins and sets?

The term "proof" refers to the method of manufacturing a coin, not to its condition. Originally proof coins were struck for presentation souvenir, exhibition and display purposes. They are now produced principally for sale to collectors who desire the finest possible specimens of the nation's current coinage.

Ideally, the proof coin is minted with a maximum of preparation and care, using highly polished dies and planchets free of imperfections. Each coin is multiple-struck at slow speed with extra pressure to bring up sharp, high relief details. Proofs are distinguished by their brilliant mirror finish, sometimes with frosted highlights and high relief rim.

Comparison of proof (top) and uncirculated coin surfaces shows such proof qualities as greater detail, sharper lines on edges of letters and numbers.

Proof set packaging has changed frequently through the years; this is a rigid plastic mounted 1982 set containing five coins, plus a special medal.

Proof sets of current U.S. coinage are produced annually at the San Francisco Mint. Each set consists of one coin of each denomination of current issue (presently 1¢, 5¢, 10¢, 25¢, 50¢), all bearing the "S" mint mark. The six coins have a face value of 91¢ and sell for $11.00 in the set form. For ordering information, contact the Numismatic Service, U.S. Mint, 55 Mint St., San Francisco, California 94175.

What does the term "proof-like" imply?

Proof-like coins have some of the visual characteristics of true proof coins, and can be produced by the first few strikes of any new production die. They are not true proof coins, since the term "proof-like" applies to the condition of a coin, not to its method of manufacture.

What is the difference between a proof set and a mint set?

A proof set consists of a set of specially manufactured specimen coins of brilliant finish, high relief and exquisite detail. A mint set is an uncirculated set of coins issued annually by the U.S. Mint. The set consists of one coin of each denomination struck for circulation at the Philadelphia and Denver Mints (presently 1¢, 5¢, 10¢, 25¢, 50¢). For ordering information, contact the Numismatic Service, U.S. Mint, 55 Mint St., San Francisco, California 94175.

What does the term "mint-sealed proof set" mean?

During the early 1960s, a "mint-sealed proof set" was, in practice, considered to be one still sealed in the original brown craft envelope as it came from the U.S. Mint. The sets were bought and sold by an incomparable act of faith, with no one actually knowing the contents of the envelope, or its condition. Later this practice was modified to the more logical insistence that the proof set still be sealed within the polyethylene-coated cellophane package enclosed in the envelope. Today the sets are sonically sealed in a rigid plastic case which can serve as a display package. Prior to mid-1955, proof coins were individually packaged in glassine coin envelopes, and these were packaged in a small box.

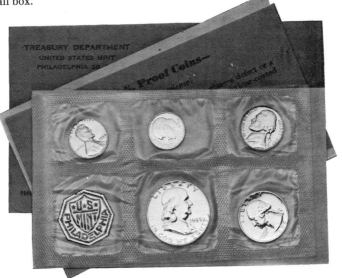

From 1955 through 1964 U.S. Mint Proof Sets were "Mint Sealed" in six pocket polyethylene-coated cellophane "flat packs," which in turn were shipped in sealed envelopes.

Is it true that the first real person to appear on an authorized U.S. coin was a foreigner?

Three of the first four were foreigners. The first identifiable person to appear on a regular issue or commemorative U.S. coin was the Italian navigator Christopher Columbus, who is generally credited with discovering America. Columbus made his appearance on the 1892 Columbian Exposition commemorative half dollar. The second person was a woman, Queen Isabella of Spain, whose portrait appears on the Columbian Exposition commemorative quarter dollar of 1893. Washington and Lafayette both appeared on the 1900 Lafayette commemorative silver dollar. This coin was the first U.S. coin to bear the portrait of an American, and the first to bear the portrait of a President of the United States.

What is a "frosted" proof coin or set?

Frosted proofs have a brilliant, mirror-like field with contrasting dull or "frosted" design and lettering. The frosting results from the difficulty of polishing the deeper recesses of the proof dies to the same degree as the more accessible areas. Frosted proofs were issued prior to 1936, and today are the frequent result of the first 15-20 strikes of a new proof die; the effect disappearing when the dies are routinely repolished.

Can you define for me the word "specie"?

The definition of specie is "coin or coined money"; colloquially, "hard money." Payment "in specie" was a constant condition of contracts in the days when the bullion value of a coin equaled or nearly approximated its face value, giving it a real worth independent of a fiscal integrity of the issuing agency.

Today, with the wealth of a nation computed in terms of resources, productivity and trade balances; with much of the world's coinage having an insignificant intrinsic value, and with the paper currency no longer backed by a pledge to redeem to value in silver or gold, the stipulation "payment in specie" has become meaningless.

Is there a Federal law against altering dates and mint marks on coins?

Federal law prohibits the possession of any coin which has been altered for the purpose of increasing its numismatic value. The mail sale of such altered coins violates the prohibition against using the mails to defraud.

What is a "matte" proof? How does it differ from a "sandblast" proof?

Both the matte and sandblast proofs have a softly lustrous granular appearance in sharp contrast to the brilliant mirror finish associated with current proofs. The matte finish is produced by pickling the planchet in dilute acid; the sandblast by pelting the planchet with sand propelled by a jet of compressed air.

What is a "special mint set"?

Special Mint Sets of United States coins were issued by the Treasury Department in 1965, 1966 and 1967 in lieu of Proof Sets and regular Mint Sets, which were discontinued due to the coin shortage of 1964. These sets included one coin of each denomination, cent through half dollar, and carried no mint mark. They were struck one at a time from specially prepared blanks, on high-tonnage presses, and handled individually after striking. They have a higher relief than regular coins, and a better appearance than the uncirculated coins in regular mint sets. The 1965 sets were housed in vinyl packets; those of 1966 and 1967 in special plastic holders. They sold for $4.00 per set.

Why was it thought necessary to find a substitute for silver in U.S. coins above the five-cent denomination?

Primarily because there was a world shortage of newly mined silver for industrial and coinage applications. The increasing artistic and industrial demand for silver — to say nothing of the vast requirement for a silver coinage — vastly exceeds the amount being mined.

Was the United States the first country to issue a clad coinage of the "sandwich" variety?

The ancient Greeks successfully fused silver to copper sheets and employed the "sandwich" for coinage purposes as early as the eighth century.

Why was a clad composition chosen for the new silverless coinage instead of pure nickel?

The clad coinage material was engineered to duplicate exactly the electrical properties of the silver coins in use. This was to insure that they would function in all existing coin vending machines, even those which accepted only those coins having the electrical properties of nearly pure silver. Converting all of the nation's vending machines to accept a pure nickel coinage would have been a lengthy and very expensive endeavor.

What is the metallic composition of the components of the clad planchet?

All of the regular-issue clad coins being struck at this time (10¢, 25¢, 50¢) have a solid copper core clad with a 75 percent copper and 25 percent nickel alloy. The uncirculated and proof Eisenhower dollars struck for souvenir and collector purposes, and the Kennedy half dollars of 1965-1970 have a core of 79 percent copper and 21 percent silver clad with a 20 percent copper and 80 percent silver alloy, giving them a total silver content of 40 percent.

By what process are the copper-nickel sheets bonded to the copper core to make planchets for the clad or sandwich coins?

It may sound like a contradiction of terms, but the three layers are literally exploded together. Sheets of the copper-nickel alloy are placed against the top and bottom surfaces of an ingot of pure copper, and fused to it by detonating an explosive material on the outer faces of the sandwich.

In what year did mint marks first appear on U.S. coins?

The mint mark first appeared on United States coinage in 1838 with the establishment of branch mints at New Orleans (O), Dahlonega (D) and Charlotte (C).

I have a coin folder which has a hole for a 1965-D Lincoln cent, yet the coin is not listed in the catalogs. Why?

The manufacturer of those folders is occasionally forced to anticipate in order to meet production and delivery schedules. Drawing on precedent, he assumed that the coins minted by the Denver Mint in 1965 would bear the traditional "D" mint mark. They did not.

A severe coin shortage developed in 1964, and an undue proportion of the blame was unjustly laid at the door of the coin collector. The mint mark was omitted from the coinage of 1965, 1966 and 1967 to reduce the specimen requirement of the collector and roll speculator. The coins struck at Denver during that three-year period cannot be distinguished from those struck at Philadelphia. The mint mark was restored in 1968, when for the first time in the nation's coinage history the mint mark for every denomination of coin appeared on the obverse.

What is a U.S. Bicentennial Coin Set?

Proof and uncirculated three-coin sets of the Bicentennial pieces consisting of 40 percent silver Washington quarter, Kennedy half and Eisenhower dollar were made available to the public on November 15, 1975. The proof set was priced at $12, and the set of uncirculated specimens at $9.

What do the 1905-S Coronet gold quarter eagles and the 1915-O Liberty Head or Barber silver half dollars have in common?

Both are excellent counterfeits of coins that never existed. The San Francisco Mint did not strike quarter eagles in 1905 and the New Orleans Mint ceased to operate as a coining facility in 1909.

Jefferson and Hamilton favored the copper half cent as a coin useful to the poor. Who argued for the inclusion of a silver half dime among the early coinage denominations, and what was his argument?

On September 28, 1790, Tom Paine, political theorist and propagandist for the American Revolution, proposed to Jefferson that a silver five-cent piece be included in the coinage system. In Paine's view, copper coins were but tokens required by convenience but having no real value. He argued that copper should be "excluded as much as possible" from the nation's coins, and that a small silver coin should be available to those who wished to minimize their possession of copper.

Early U.S. Mint Coins

As the American colonies were once British possessions, what is the reason that we did not adopt the Sterling currency system, as did most other countries which subsequently emerged from British denomination?

The reason was not, as some suggest, to disassociate the United States from everything English. The Founding Fathers adopted substantial portions of English law, religion, and social and political philosophy.

Despite its arbitrary and cumbersome complexities, the Sterling standard would quite possibly have been retained had British America remained a colony of the Crown, although efforts to express its value components in terms of the more prevalent Spanish coinage had already created a chaos of intercolony exchange rates. The adoption of a currency system more suited to the economic reality of the colonies was facilitated by the philosophical atmosphere of the War for Independence, which conditioned self-reliant men to cast off the shackles of tradition and initiate changes with little nostalgia for customs of the past.

England had never furnished the colonies with more than token quantities of Sterling-standard currency. The coins of the colonies were English, Spanish, French, Dutch and private issues. An effort was made by the various colonial governments to express their values in terms of Sterling denominations, but the assigned values varied from colony to colony, making intercolonial commerce a horror of reconciliation and adjustment. The Spanish dollar, being divided into eight equal parts, contained an inherent suggestion of a more logical system. A decimal currency with subdivisions of tenths and hundredths, wherein the American and Spanish dollars would be equivalent units, was both desirable and logical, and the intellectual climate was equitable for the inauguration of change.

Who formulated the original plans for our system of decimal currency?

In 1780, Gouverneur Morris, a member of the Continental Congress, wrote a series of essays containing suggestions for the projected financial system of the new nation. These proposals attracted the attention of Robert Morris, the superintendent of finance, and he appointed Gouverneur Morris to serve as his assistant. During the following four years, Gouverneur Morris laid the basis for much of the national currency system. The Morris unit was based on 1/1440 of a dollar, and was calculated to agree with all different valuations of the Spanish milled dollar, as then stipulated by the various states, without a fraction.

Thomas Jefferson agreed with the fundamental Morris suggestions, but disagreed with Morris' complicated money unit. In 1784, he suggested a simple dollar unit with decimal divisions of ten. In this, he was later supported by President George Washington.

In 1791, Secretary of the Treasury Alexander Hamilton concurred with the decimal proposal, and called also for the use of both gold and silver in the nation's monetary system. The proposals of Hamilton were adopted on April 2, 1792.

Of the various coin denominations which have circulated in this country through the years, which ones were provided for initially?

The Congressional Act of April 2, 1792, provided "that the money of the United States should be expressed in dollars or units, dismes or tenths, cents or hundredths, and milles or thousandths, a disme being the tenth part of a dollar, a cent the hundredth part of a dollar, a mille the thousandth part of a dollar . . ."

The denominations specified by the act were: Gold Eagle or $10, Gold Half Eagle or $5, Gold Quarter Eagle or $2.50, Silver Dollar or $1, Silver Half Dollar or $0.50, Silver Quarter Dollar or $0.25, Silver Disme or $0.10, Silver Half Disme or $0.05, Copper Cent or $0.01, and Copper Half Cent or $0.005.

The act further provided that "every fifteen pounds weight of pure silver shall be of equal value in all payments with one pound weight of pure gold, and so in all proportion . . ."

How long has the United States operated a mint?

The first U.S. Mint was authorized by Congress on April 2, 1792, and has operated since October, 1792. The first coin produced in the first mint, a pattern half disme (5 cents), was struck in July, 1792, while the Mint was still under construction. Fifteen hundred specimens were struck from personal silver plate provided by George Washington. It is believed that Martha Washington modeled this first coin of the U.S. Mint.

Aside from patterns, the striking of half cents and cents began in 1793; half dimes, half dollars and silver dollars in 1794; dimes and quarter dollars in 1796; $5 and $10 gold in 1795; $2.50 gold in 1796.

Where was the first United States Mint located?

The building housing the first mint of the United States was erected on Seventh Street near Arch in Philadelphia, with the cornerstone being laid on July 31, 1792. The power for the mint was provided by two oxen, and it was

Smallest monetary unit ever issued in the United States was the half cent, minted from 1793 through 1857.

guarded by a three-dollar dog called Nero. The United States has continuously operated a mint in Philadelphia since that time, coining money at the initial site for some forty years.

The original mint was the first public building erected by authority of the Federal Government.

I have often read about a "chain cent". What is it?

The term "chain" or "link" cent refers to the first regular-issue cent, struck in 1793. The principal device of the reverse design of this cent, a circular chain of fifteen links, was intended to symbolize the solidarity of the states then in the Union. The public, however, thought otherwise, and condemned the chain device as symbolic of bondage. The chain was replaced by a wreath in the latter part of 1793. Chain cents are quite scarce, and command a substantial premium.

Why are there such a number of die varieties of large cents?

Early dies were hand engraved individually; human imperfection assured that no two dies of any denomination would be completely alike. Today, one master die creates all working dies in its own image. Varieties of the same cause and latitude existed in all denominations of early coinage.

Why was the large cent the only United States coin minted during 1816?

The machinery for producing coins was damaged by a fire in January of 1816. Resumption of operations probably concentrated upon production of the large cent because it was essential to a growing commerce and the only U.S. coin of the time not supplemented by foreign coins that enjoyed legal-tender status. The large cent would have also been the easiest to produce under emergency conditions, since the cent planchets were purchased outside the Mint and were not dependent upon the operation of the Mint's rolling mill.

I have noticed that United States coins after 1817 have fewer minor varieties in design. Why is this?

After the fire of 1816, the mint was provided with a large brick building, and the worn and damaged equipment was replaced with new and improved machinery. The mechanical improvements enabled better and more uniform die cutting and hardening of the dies. More uniform and longer-lasting dies could only result in less varieties.

Of particular interest to numismatists, the mechanical screw-type coin presses were replaced by hydraulic presses capable of exerting a greater and more uniformly applied pressure. An immediate consequence was the production of proofs and medals in 1817.

Why are early half dollars relatively easy to obtain, many in real nice condition, while other coins of the late 1700s and early 1800s are hard to find in nice condition?

Free circulation of early United States gold and silver coins was greatly hindered by speculators. Worn Spanish dollars of reduced weight were exchanged for the newly minted dollars of the United States, with the heavier coin being exported and lost to local commerce. The gold coins were undervalued in relation to the standard of European commercial centers and were melted for bullion. The 1794-1834 coinage of half dimes, dimes and quarter dollars was negligible. The only U.S. coin readily available for large transactions, bank reserves and foreign payment was the half dollar. Being regarded as bullion, and being mainly transferred from bank to bank, they were subjected to very little wear, which accounts for the good supply and superior condition of these half dollars today.

I have an 1818 half dollar with lettering on the edge. Does this edge make it scarce?

Half dollars had FIFTY CENTS OR HALF A DOLLAR lettered on the edge until 1836, after which the edge of the coin was reeded. None of the half dollars of this period are plentiful, but the scarcity is unrelated to the type of edge.

What was the idea behind having a lettered edge on coins?

In the day of bullion coinage, many people could not resist the temptation to shave or file a few grains of gold or silver from the edge of each coin that passed through their hands. Lettering, reeding or ornamenting the edge made the practice more difficult by readily betraying the coins that had been depreciated in this common, but unlawful, manner.

What American coin was popularly known as the "Blowsy Barmaid"?

None of the Liberty Heads utilized on the large copper cents challenged existing standards of artistic excellence, and were known by such uncomplimentary names as "Silly Head" and "Booby Head." The public was particularly unappreciative of the 1808-1814 Classic Head type which presented "a sleepy-looking Liberty turbaned with a diaphanous nightcloth," and promptly dubbed her the "Blowsy Barmaid."

Recently while viewing the exhibits at a coin convention, I saw a half dime of the late 1700s. It was called Uncirculated and valued in excess of $5,000 although it was obviously defaced, as though someone had filed on it. How can a damaged coin command such a premium?

Many early U.S. coins, particularly the higher denomination silver and gold issues, bear surface markings which are similar to those you observed. These markings can be file marks, as you indicated, and are technically known as adjustment marks. The coin you saw was probably struck from a planchet which inspectors had found to be overweight. It was "adjusted" to standard by removing the excess weight with a file. When the planchet was subsequently struck into a coin the pressure applied was insufficient to completely obliterate the file markings. Had the planchet been found to be underweight, it would have been melted.

Were the 1793 cents and half cents the first coins to be struck by the United States Mint?

No, but they were the first regular-issue coins produced by the United States Mint. The first coins of the United States to be produced with Mint equipment and personnel and under the direction of Mint Director David Rittenhouse were the 1792 half disme and disme. They were struck in the

basement of a saw-maker named Harper on or about July 13, 1792, at the request of President Washington and on planchets made from silver plate provided by Martha Washington. It is presumed that the bust of Liberty featured on these coins represents Martha Washington, copied in profile from a painting by Trumbull. If so, she has the distinction of being the first American citizen ever to appear on a U.S. coin. Washington distributed the coins to friends in Virginia and Europe. There was no further coining of dismes and half dismes of this type. The 1792 half disme is considered to be the first pattern piece made by the Mint.

The first pieces actually struck at the new Mint building were silver-center cent patterns produced on December 17, 1792, from dies prepared by Henry Voight. These unusual cents had a plug of silver valued at three-quarters of a cent in the center of a copper planchet valued at one-quarter of a cent, the intent being to manufacture a cent of the requisite intrinsic value but of a smaller size than the huge coppers authorized by Congress. Copper-silver cents were also produced in which the silver was directly alloyed with the copper, in effect producing the billon cent Jefferson advocated.

I recently saw an illustration of a large copper piece of the United States which was dated 1792, and had on obverse a rather attractive Liberty Head and the legend: LIBERTY PARENT OF SCIENCE AND INDUSTRY. Is this a Mint coin or a token?

It is a pattern cent made at the Mint in 1792 from dies produced by Robert Birch, whose name appears on the obverse. One variety of this proposed cent carries the abbreviations "G.W.Pt." (George Washington President) directly above the bottom rim on reverse. Another states the value fractionally as 1/100, as it would later appear on the regular-issue 1793 cents. The Birch cent patterns are known with plain edge and with edge inscribed TO BE ESTEEMED BE USEFUL.

The first regular-issue United States quarter wasn't struck until 1796. Have any quarter patterns struck prior to that date survived?

Comparatively few pattern pieces are known that were struck before 1836. There is, however, an interesting piece dated 1792 which bears a nude female bust on the obverse, and the word LIBERTY; and has on the reverse an eagle standing on a globe and the legend UNITED STATES OF AMERICA, all encircled by a ring of 87 small stars. At one time it was thought that this piece was a pattern for a gold half eagle, but its size and the fact that the Mint was planning an early quarter production favors the conclusion that this pattern (actually a die trial with a wide rim) was prepared with the quarter in mind.

Is it true that the early dimes bore no mark of value?

The value of the pattern dimes and half dimes struck in 1792 was spelled out as DISME and HALF DISME. From 1796, the first year regular issues

were coined, through 1807 the dime carried no mark of value. A value designation first appeared on regular-issue dimes in 1809, when the value was stated as 10 C. A mark of value first appeared on the half dime in 1829, and on the quarter dollar in 1804.

I understand that during the first 20 years or so of the Mint's existence only about a million dimes were minted. Why weren't more coined?

There was no demand for the minting of low-denomination silver coins during the early years of the republic. Small Spanish silver coins were in good supply, and they were neither brought to the Mint for recoining, melted by silversmiths nor exported because, being excessively worn, their face value significantly exceeded their intrinsic worth.

The quarter dollar was also a denomination seldom requested by those who deposited silver with Mint for coining. The first quarters weren't struck until 1796, and they were issued in only six different years until 1818. It wasn't until 1835 that more than a million examples were struck in any one year.

I have heard it said that one of the early engravers employed by the Mint was a slave. Is there any truth in this?

John Reich, assistant engraver of the Mint from April 1, 1807, to March 31, 1817, was a German bondsman freed by a Mint official. Although officially Robert Scot's assistant, he redesigned and engraved every denomination of coin issued during his tenure.

Cents from 1856

What was the reasoning behind the change from the large copper cent to the small cent in 1857, and the accompanying decision to drop the half-cent?

The large cent, although a useful denomination, was never popular with the people because of its excessive size and weight; nor with Treasury officials because, in relation to its face value, it was expensive to produce.

The half-cent, being essentially an unnecessary coin, was even more unpopular. Many banks considered it a nuisance and refused to handle it.

I had always assumed that the term "white cents" referred to the steel cents of 1943, but my brother maintains that the term refers to cents of the 1850s and 1860s. Who is right?

Your brother. "White cents" is the term applied to the Flying Eagle cents of 1856-1858, and the Indian Head cents of 1859-1864. They were struck of a metal which contained 88 parts copper to 12 parts nickel, thus giving them a light or white appearance.

Where is the "L" located on Indian Head cents of 1864 and what is its significance?

The "L" is located on the bonnet ribbon of the Indian's headdress, immediately below the last feather. It is somewhat hidden, and can best be seen if the coin is slightly turned so that the Indian faces the observer. The letter is the initial of James Longacre, the coin's designer. All Indian Head cents after 1864 have this initial on them.

I have noticed that the initials V.D.B. appear on the reverse of some 1909 Lincoln cents, and am wondering why they do not appear on all of them, and are not on any of the other dates?

The initials V.D.B. refer to the designer of the Lincoln cent, Victor D. Brenner. At the time the new Lincoln cent was released in 1909, the public objection to "defacing a coin for personal gain or reputation" was so great that the initials were removed. In 1918 the initials were restored, but in very small letters at the base of Lincoln's shoulder on the obverse, and they have remained to the present time.

How can I determine if I am looking at a genuine 1914-D Lincoln cent or one with an altered date?

The majority of altered-date 1914-D cents are made by removing part of the second "4" of 1944-D cents. Cents altered in this manner can be detected by placing another cent vertically on the coin being tested, placing the left edge of the vertical cent against the right loop of the "9" of date. If the 1914-D is genuine, only the upright and right crosslet extension of the "4" will remain visible. If any portion of the left extension of the crosslet is visible, the 1914-D is an altered 1944-D. There will also be an extra wide space between the "1" and "9" and the "D" will be larger and positioned higher on an altered 1944-D cent than on a genuine 1914-D.

Altered-date 1914-D cents are also made by adding a "D" to 1914 cents, and by replacing the "S" of 1914-S cents with a "D". In fact any coin with a date ending with the numeral "4" and bearing a "D" mint mark can be, and has been, altered to a 1914-D. The removal of a mint mark or date component will invariably leave traces of the filing or burnishing. The addition of a detail will always leave traces of discoloration resulting from the application of heat. Genuine 1914-D cents do not bear the initials V.D.B. which were removed from the cent in 1909 and restored in 1918 to a point on shoulder truncation. If the date has been altered on any cent minted after 1917, the shoulder truncation may reveal the initials, or evidence that they have been removed.

According to the mint report, no 1922 cents were coined at any mint except Denver, but I notice that the books and dealers offer 1922 plain, or, I assume, Philadelphia, cents. How can this be?

What is advertised as a 1922 plain cent is nothing more than a 1922-D cent struck from a worn die in which the D punch filled in, resulting in no D, or but faint traces of one, raised upon the coin.

A few years ago the white wartime cents were easily found in circulation. However, I have not seen one during the past few years. Are they now rare?

While the wartime steel cents are seldom encountered in circulation today, they are not rare; nor is there any reason to suppose that they will be within the meaningful future. Intrigued by its novelty, many noncollectors saved the steel cent during the war years. Many of these accumulations ended up in the hands of dealers and neighborhood collectors. Brilliant uncirculated specimens could appreciate substantially in value, for the zinc-plated coin was extremely vulnerable to atmospheric solvents, but the "processed" steel cent will be in good supply for years to come.

I have been told by many collectors that the cents of 1944 and 1945 were struck from metal which was recovered from expended military shell cases. Is this correct?

Yes. The coloring of these coins is a little different, tending toward the yellow shades, but the coin proved satisfactory in every respect. These "shell case" cents were popularly received by a public that had rejected the steel cent issues of 1943.

I have noticed that on some 1955 cents struck at the Philadelphia Mint, the features on the obverse appear to be double struck. Can you explain why the reverse features do not also appear to be double struck.

Small quantity of 1955 Philadelphia cents were struck from die with doubled obverse, a result of die shifting out of alignment between successive strikes from the master die, or hub.

The 1955 cent of which you speak is not really a double strike. This coin was struck in a single impression from a die which had been struck by a hub which was not in alignment on each strike. Working dies are made from a positive hub, by a process which necessitates several strikes, and if either the die or hub is not in perfect alignment on each succeeding strike, a doubling of features will result.

As the obverse die is made at a different time, but by the same process, this explains why the reverse features are normal, although the same double die feature is possible on the reverse.

All of the Lincoln cents with the Memorial on the reverse which I have noticed spell the "OF" in "UNITED STATES OF AMERICA" with a small "o". Is this an error?

No. The small "o" was deliberate on the part of the engraver Frank Gasparro, whose initials appear at the base of the steps to the right of the Memorial. This has been done on a number of U.S. coins, including the Franklin half-dollar and several commemoratives.

Is it easy to distinguish between the large and small dates on 1960 cents?

LARGE   SMALL

It isn't difficult once you have seen the coins or good illustrations of them. The mental picture most viewers retain is of the chubby compactness of the small date 6 and its shorter tail. Other differences to look for are that the top of the 1 aligns with the top of the 9 in the small-date variety, and the numerals are somewhat closer together in the large-date variety.

Can the large and small date varieties of the 1970-S cent be readily distinguished? How were the varieties created?

LARGE   SMALL

The most obvious difference in the date varieties is that on the large date the "O" and the loop of the "9" extend above the "7". According to a spokesman for the Bureau of the Mint, the varieties were created when an engraver sharpened the date features in the master die from which the working dies are produced.

Is it true that a little white girl modeled the Indian head on the Indian Head cent?

One of the more enduring of numismatic legends holds that the model for the cent was Sarah Longacre, the engraver's 12-year-old daughter, wearing the ceremonial bonnet of a visiting Indian chief. However, Longacre's sketches would seem to indicate that his inspiration was the goddess Venus in Indian attire.

I have been told that 1864 bronze Indian Head cents with the "L" can be identified without directly verifying the presence of the "L". How can this be?

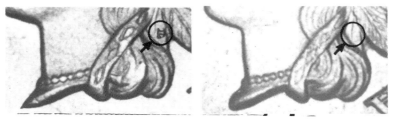

The tip of the bust is pointed on the variety with the "L"; rounded on the one without it.

What is meant by Variety 1 and Variety 2 of the 1886 Indian Head cent?

On the Variety 1 cent the last feather of the bonnet points to between I and C of AMERICA; on Variety 2 it points to between C and A. All of the Indian Head cents after 1886 are Variety 2.

Are "cents" and "pennies" the same thing?

It is true that, due to our English heritage, the terms are used interchangeably in the United States, but they are not the same thing. "Cent" is from the Latin centesimus, meaning "a hundredth part." In our coinage laws, the cent is the hundredth part of the dollar. The British "penny" was formerly valued at 240 per pound sterling. Since the British change to a decimal system coinage in 1971, the "new pence or penny" is valued at 100 per pound. At this writing, the pound is worth approximately $1.30 U.S.

I thought it was required by law that each of the coins of the United States bear "an impression emblematic of Liberty." The word "Liberty" is plainly evident on the large copper cents, the Indian Heads and the Lincolns. Where is it on the Flying Eagle cent?

LIBERTY does not appear on the Flying Eagle cent, nor is it to be found on the two-cent piece, the silver three-cent piece or the Shield nickel. Apparently it was felt that the primary device of the Flying Eagle cent, an eagle in free flight, adequately symbolized the ideal of liberty.

I have read that during the Civil War people hoarded copper-nickel cents hoping to profit from their bullion value. Is that the only reason why the composition of the cent was changed to bronze in 1864?

A number of other considerations also influenced the decision. Nickel was expensive to procure and difficult to alloy with copper because of its high melting point. Its hardness was very destructive to dies. Treasury officials were favorably impressed by the public acceptance of light-weight, low-value copper Civil War tokens, and reasoned that the cent could be made lighter and of a cheaper metal without adversely affecting its acceptance.

Is it true that one of the regular-issue coins of the United States carries a representation of the same person on both sides?

The Lincoln-Memorial cent has a bust of Lincoln on the obverse and a seated Lincoln in the Lincoln Memorial on reverse. This coin also carries the initials of two engravers, Victor D. Brenner and Frank Gasparro.

Why were only 1,000 Flying Eagle cents minted in 1856, the year the type was first struck?

Authority to produce the Flying Eagle cent wasn't forthcoming until February 21, 1857. An estimated 1,000 (some place the figure much higher) Flying Eagle pattern cents were struck in 1856 as pattern, ostensibly to provide the Congress with specimens for evaluation of the proposal to change coinage standards to authorize the small cent.

I have always thought the Flying Eagle cent to be one of the most attractive coins ever issued by the United States. Why was it discontinued so abruptly?

It would appear that the public didn't share your appraisal of this truly venturesome coin, the design of which was adapted from the powerful flying eagle of the 1836-1839 Gobrecht pattern dollars. Allegedly, production ceased after two years because of official objection to the coin being popularly known as the "Buzzard" cent.

Wasn't Lincoln the first real person to appear on a regular-issue coin of the United States?

Lincoln's appearance on the cent in 1909 marked the first appearance of a identifiable person, and the first appearance of a U.S. President, on our regular-issue coinage.

Which of the branch mints was the first to coin U.S. cents?

The San Francisco Mint began striking bronze Indian Head cents in 1908.

When were the first copper plated zinc cents struck and placed in circulation?

The first zinc cents were struck on Dec. 17, 1981 — dated 1982 — at the Mint's satellite facility at the West Point Bullion Depository. As these pieces are without mintmark, they are indistinguishable from those subsequently produced at the Philadelphia Mint. The first of this new generation of zinc cents began entering in circulation in mid-January. Late in 1982 cent production at Denver was also converted from the old copper based standard to the new zinc based issue. Commencing in 1983 and subsequently, all cents have been struck from pure copper plated planchets with a core of 99.2% zinc and 0.8% copper.

How can you tell the difference between the bronze and zinc cent strikes of 1982?

There is a perceptible difference in the weight of the two versions — the bronze cent weighs 3.11 grams, or 24.4% heavier than the 2.5 grams weight of the copper plated zinc cents — which can actually be detected as the coins are individually held in one's hands. Also the copper plated zinc cents, particularly those minted through the first few months, often carry dark surface discoloration and display surface bubbling, both of which are uncharacteristic of their bronze sisters.

Were proof cents of 1982 struck on both bronze and copper plated zinc planchets?

No, all 1982 proof cents were struck on bronze planchets; commencing in 1983 all proof cents were struck on copper plated zinc planchets.

I understand there are both large and small date varieties of 1982 cents. Can I identify bronze and copper plated zinc cents of that year by a study of this feature?

Small Date - 1982 - Bronze   Large Date - 1982-D - Plated Zinc

Only from the standpoint that if you have a 1982-D small date cent, it will be struck on a copper plated zinc planchet. Large date 1982-D cents were struck in both metals, as were both the large and small date 1982 Philadelphia offerings. All proofs were struck from large date dies.

Can you tell my how many basic types of small cents there are, and the years they were minted?

Flying Eagle	1857-1858
Indian Head (Copper-Nickel, Laurel Reverse)	1859
Indian Head (Copper-Nickel, Oak Reverse)	1860-1864
Indian Head (Bronze)	1864-1909
Lincoln Head	1909-1942, 1946-1958
Lincoln Head (Zinc Plated Steel)	1943
Lincoln Head (Shell Case Copper)	1944-1945
Lincoln Head (Memorial Reverse)	1959-1982
Lincoln Head (Copper Coated Zinc)	1982 to Date

Nickels from 1866

Why did the United States begin coining nickel five-cent pieces in 1866, when they had been and still were coining silver half-dimes?

War, with its vast expenditure of money and priority for non-consumer goods, traditionally produces inflation. Early in 1862, all metallic currency began to disappear from circulation. Citizens, anticipating an increase in bullion values, began hoarding gold, silver, even copper, coins. The silver half-dime, an essential denomination of everyday commerce, was among the first to vanish. It was thought that a five-cent piece of nonprecious metal (75% copper, 25% nickel) would discourage hoarding and satisfy an essential need.

What does the term "racketeer nickel" mean?

The first Liberty Head nickels minted early in 1883 bore, on reverse, only a large letter "V" to indicate value. The coin's similarity in size and weight to a five-dollar gold piece prompted some opportunists to gold plate it, reed the edge with a private tooling device, and pass it as a new type five-dollar gold piece. These gold-plated nickels are known to collectors as "racketeer nickels." Later in 1883, the design of the Liberty Head nickel was altered by adding the word "CENTS" below the wreath on reverse.

How many of the Liberty Head type nickels were struck in 1913?

No 1913 Liberty Head nickels were *officially* struck. The five known specimens were illegally struck, almost certainly at the Mint and with authentic dies, by private initiative. All five coins are presently accounted for. By established legal precedent, they could be confiscated by the government at any time as unauthorized coinage.

Although not an official U.S. coin issue, five specimens of the 1913 Liberty head nickel were struck, all of which are accounted for. Sometimes reported as number six is a copper strike of the 1913 Indian head type.

When they first surfaced in 1920, they were housed in a case with a bronze 1913 Buffalo nickel. The presence of six coins in the case is the basis for the incorrect assumption that all six were Liberty Heads.

I have been told by some people that the three-legged variety of the 1937-D Buffalo nickel was created when the engraver making the die made a mistake and omitted a leg. Others say the variety was created when that area of the die became filled with a foreign material. Who has given me the correct answer?

The first answer is certainly incorrect, and, in the view of some authorities, the second (die clogging) cannot explain why the rest of the relief is reduced in circumference and height. The semi-official explanation of a Mint employee is that the variety was created "when the die was ground down to remove injuries sustained during its accidental clash with the obverse die." Whatever the cause, the oddity caught the collector's fancy. Curiously, the 1930-S with eight legs and the 1935-D with two legs have been all but ignored.

Are the so-called restored date Buffalo nickels considered valuable as collectors' items?

Not by serious collectors. The worn dates are made temporarily visible by an application of acid. The disappearance of the "restored" date after the coin has been passed off on an uninformed or novice collector can be of no possible benefit to the hobby.

Why is a coin struck as recently as the 1950-D nickel so hard to find?

The mintage of a circulating coin is not determined by consideration of collector needs. The 1950-D nickel had the lowest mintage (2,630,030) of any year or mint of regular issue Jefferson nickel coinage to date. A significant percentage of the mintage was immediately set aside in uncirculated rolls by collectors and speculators, so few specimens ever reached circulation, accounting for the narrow spread in values between uncirculated and circulated quality examples today.

What is a "silver nickel"?

The term is applied to the wartime five-cent piece (1942-45) composed of 56% copper, 35% silver and 9% manganese. Because nickel imparts great strength and corrosion resistance to steel, and because the United States must import most of its nickel, it was decided to reserve the stockpile of that metal normally employed in the production of five-cent pieces for the use of war industry. To indicate the change of alloy, the mint mark was made larger and placed above the dome of Monticello, and for the first time in the nation's coinage history, the letter "P" was used to designate domestic coins struck at the Philadelphia Mint.

I have a 1944 silver nickel without a mint mark. Is it valuable?

It is a counterfeit, thought to have originated in New Jersey. The counterfeiter evidently prepared his mold from coins of two different dates, using the reverse of a prewar nickel struck at the Philadelphia Mint, thus producing a passable copy of a nonexistent coin.

Is it true the Jefferson nickel was designed in open competition outside the Mint?

The design for the Jefferson nickel originated from a completely open competition for a $1000 prize. The winning design was submitted by Felix Schlag, a rather obscure sculptor at the time. His initials "FS" were added below the bust beginning in 1966.

I recently found a naturally dark (not tarnished) Jefferson nickel. What caused the unusual color? Is it valuable?

Off-color Jefferson nickels are not uncommon, and are known in hues ranging from smoky blue through deep purple to black. The natural discoloration is caused by an incorrect alloy mix containing significantly too much copper. Some collectors are attracted to them, as some prefer toned proof coins, and will pay a small premium for them.

Is the Indian on the Indian Head or Buffalo nickel a real person?

Three of them. It is generally agreed that Chief Two Moons, a Cheyenne, modeled the forehead; Chief John Big Tree, an Iroquois, the nose and mouth; Chief Iron Tail, a Sioux, the chin and throat. Black Diamond, a bison living at the New York Zoological Gardens, served as the model for the "buffalo" on the coin.

Why is the buffalo standing on a mound on some 1913 nickels, and on a straight ground line on others?

Soon after the new design was placed in production, it was realized that the "mound" design was causing striking difficulties, would be subject to rapid wear in circulation, and provided a coin that tended not to work well in vending machines because of its thickness. Both deficiencies were corrected by sinking the surface of the coin and displaying the statement of value there, beneath the "straight ground line," which is essentially a protective bar.

I have some nickels dated 1942, 1943, 1944 and 1945 which appear to be of a much darker color than normal. Each of these coins also has a large letter above the dome of Monticello on the reverse. Are these coins rare?

Your coins are not rare, but all are significantly more valuable than most of the other Jefferson nickels which immediately preceded and followed them. The reason they are more valuable is that they contain a high percentage of silver, the same property which makes them a darker color. Nickels of these years struck with this silver content, in substitution for nickel, are distinguished by the presence of the large letters P, D and S for mint marks over Monticello's dome, this being the only instance that a U.S. coin minted at Philadelphia has carried a mint mark.

Nearly 60-percent of the nickel production for 1942 consisted of coins bearing a 35-percent silver content in replacement for a like amount of nickel previously used. The substitution was used because nickel was a critical war material and silver was considered rather valueless at the time. When the bullion value for silver hit the 90-cents per ounce range in the early 1960s, these nickels started trading at a premium based on the value of their metal content, and people quickly found that it would be to their advantage to remove them from circulation.

When did the motto "In God We Trust" first appear on the nickel?

The first use of the motto occurred on the 1866-1883 Shield nickel. It did not appear on either the Liberty Head or the Indian Head (Buffalo) nickels, but was reintroduced in 1938 with the appearance of the Jefferson nickel.

During 1866 and part of 1867, the reverse of the Shield nickel was designed with 13 rays positioned between 13 stars encircling a large numeral 5. This design wasn't unattractive. Why were the rays removed?

Various reasons have been advanced, none of an official nature. One opinion holds that the rays produced a cluttered effect which the public found unattractive. Another, and more logical, suggestion is that the hardness of the nickel planchets caused dies to break after about 20,000 strikes, and the rays were removed to simplify the overall coin design, thus prolonging the life of working dies.

When authority to mint a nickel five-cent piece was legislated in 1866, was the coin a needed and logical substitute for the silver half dime?

A nonsilver five-cent coin was required at the time to serve as a replacement for the silver half dime which, along with other gold and silver coins, had been driven from circulation by the post-Civil War suspension of specie payment. A five-cent coin that would remain in circulation was also required to speed the retirement of unpopular fractional currency notes of ten-cent denomination and less. Logically, a nickel five-cent piece was a curious coin to produce in the aftermath of a successful campaign to mint cents of bronze instead of copper-nickel that had been largely based on the argument that striking hard copper-nickel cent planchets had worn out the Mint's coin presses and prematurely broken a fantastic number of expensive dies.

Miscellaneous U.S. Coins

Is it possible to distinguish between the large and small motto two-cent pieces of 1864 without the aid of a magnifying glass?

A difference in the shape of the letters O and D in the motto IN GOD WE TRUST can be detected without a visual aid. On the small motto variety, the inside space of these letters is wider and round in shape. On the large motto, the space is perceptibly narrower and oval-like in shape.

People have told me that the three-cent denomination was introduced into our coinage system because of the postal situation at the time. Could you explain this for me?

There were two principal reasons for the introduction of the three-cent piece.

In 1851 letter postage was reduced from 5¢ to 3¢. It was thought that purchase of the three-cent stamp could be more conveniently made with a three-cent coin than with the large copper cents.

The discovery of gold in California in 1849 dramatically increased the supply of the metal, and resulted in a drop in the price of gold in relation to that of silver. The intrinsic value of silver coins rose above their face value, that is they became worth more as bullion than as money. They were hoarded or exported to the detriment of trade. The silver three-cent piece was made with a lowered fineness and an intrinsic value of 86 percent of face to discourage hoarding and provide a coin for trade.

I have seen in advertisements references to three types of silver three-cent pieces. How do you distinguish between them?

No Lines Around Star
1851-1853

Olive Sprig And Bundle Of Arrows
Added For Issues Of 1854-1873

Three Outlines To Star
1854-1859

Two Outlines To Star
1859-1873

The type of 1851-53 has no lines bordering the six-pointed obverse star, and does not have olive sprig above nor bundle of arrows below the reverse Roman numeral III. The type of 1854-58 has three outlines to star, olive sprig above numeral III and bundle of three arrows below. The type of 1859-73 has two outlines to star and olive sprig and arrows similar to type of 1854-58.

My teacher told us that the first copper coins produced at the U.S. Mint weren't coins at all, but tokens. Is she right?

The coinage bill enacted on April 2, 1792, provided for a token coinage of copper cents and half cents. Minor copper coins weren't given legal tender status until April 22, 1864, when the cent was made legal tender up to ten cents and the two-cent piece up to twenty cents.

What is the history surrounding the short life of the twenty-cent piece?

The why of the twenty-cent piece is still debated: It was envisioned as a means of preventing short-changing which resulted from the Western tradition of pricing items according to the Spanish "bit" (12½ ¢); or it was the first step in the implementation of Senator Sarent's proposal to mint all coins above the nickel in units of tens, that is to mint a twenty-cent and forty-cent coin and eliminate the quarter and half dollar; or it was an attempt by the senators from the silver states to legislate another guaranteed market for silver.

The coin was soon discontinued because although its edge was plain, its value prominently stated, and its reverse eagle faced in the opposite direction, it was in practice confused with the quarter dollar. Introduced in 1875, it was minted for general issue only that year and in early 1876; proof specimens were struck in 1877 and 1878, after which time the issue was discontinued.

If the half-cent was "unnecessary," why was it initially included in the nation's coinage program?

When the United States Mint became operational, the most widely used currency in the nation was the Spanish dollar and its subsidiary parts, which remained legal tender until 1857. Although both the Spanish and U.S. dollars were equivalent to 100 cents, U.S. standard, their minor coins were computed by different fractional standards. That is, while 2 reales Spanish equaled 25¢ U.S., the 1 real was equal to 12½ ¢, and the ½ real had an accepted value at the retail level of 6½ ¢. Hamilton proposed the half-cent piece to prevent the poor from being systematically bilked when making purchases or receiving change in U.S. coin.

Can you tell me why the tiny silver three-cent piece was popularly called a "trime"?

No. The word isn't in "Webster's Collegiate Dictionary," but "trine" is. The definition of trine is three-fold or triple.

Why did the United States stop minting a three-cent piece?

Three-cent pieces were introduced in 1851 as silver coins, under the same Mar. 3, 1851, law that cut the nation's postage rate from 5-cents per ounce to 3-cents. An anomaly in a decimal-standard coinage, it was intended as an issue that would faciliatate the purchase. Never a popular issue, with the onset of the Civil War silver three-cent pieces all but totally disappeared from the scene. In 1865 three-cent coinage was reinstroduced on a large scale as a nickel coin that would circulate alongside and replace a fractional currency note issue of like denomination. Although minting of the nickel version continued until 1889, the quantities produced annually were quite small after the early 1870s when the basic postage was revised downward again. The general revision of coinage laws in 1873 had eliminated the silver three-cent piece.

Why was the nickel three-cent piece introduced into our coinage while silver three-cent pieces were still being minted?

The hoarding of metallic currency during the Civil War forced the government to issue fractional currency. A large number of three-cent notes were issued early in 1863. The nickel interests saw an opportunity to push for a nickel three-cent piece with a low intrinsic value discourage hoarding, that would be used for redeeming the three-cent notes, following elimination of nickel content in the cent in 1864. It was introduced in 1865.

The two-cent piece of 1864-73 had a short production run and comparatively small mintages. Why was it produced?

The two-cent piece was issued in 1864 in an attempt to alleviate the exasperating coin shortage caused by the hoarding of coins in the Civil War years. It was briefly necessary and readily accepted, but need for it diminished with the end of hostilities and it was discontinued.

When did the motto IN GOD WE TRUST first appear on our coinage?

The two-cent piece of 1864 was the first U.S. coin to bear this now familiar motto.

What was the smallest coin the United States ever minted?

The half-cent piece (1793-1857) had the lowest face value of any U.S. coin. The silver three-cent piece (1851-73) was the smallest in physical size.

Half Dimes and Dimes from 1837

How did the 1844 dime gain the tag "Orphan Annie"?

Only 72,500 dimes were minted in 1844, but nobody noticed. Coin collectors were as rare as Greeley's union printers, there were no speculators wearing slide rules calibrated to predict instant and infinite profits. Attrition, abetted by collector neglect, took a great toll of the small mintage. In 1930 (so the story goes) a Kansas City collector discovered that the 1844 dime was even more rare than its mintage indicated, and that this rarity wasn't reflected by its market premium. He dubbed it Orphan Annie because "the coin had no buyers, and was just an orphan in the coin world."

Can you explain the significance of the arrows near the date on some 1853 dimes?

The arrows were added to the dimes of 1853-1855 to denote a decrease in the weight of the dime from 41.25 to 38.4 grains. Proportionate changes in the half dime, quarter and half were denoted in the same manner. The arrows were again employed in 1873-74 to denote an increase in weight to 38.58 grains.

Can you explain what is meant by a 1942/41 dime? Is it a dime with a dual date?

The 1942/41 dime is a major mint error produced by a production die which, in preparation, had been given one blow with a 1941 hub and then, by some accident, finished with a 1942 hub. The result was a working die with a 2 imprinted over the last 1 of the date. An unknown number of dimes were struck with this die and released before the error was detected. As only the last numeral of the date was affected, technically this dime should be referred to as a 1942/1 dime.

What is meant by the term "Micro S 1945-S dime"?

The "S" mint mark on some of the 1945-S dimes is significantly smaller than that appearing on normal 1945 dimes struck by the San Francisco Mint. This was caused by the "S" having been stamped on the working die with a smaller type punch than normally employed.

I have always held the opinion that the Roosevelt dime was introduced in 1946 to commemorate the passing from the scene of the president who had the longest tenure in the history of the country. Is this the accepted theory?

Popularity is greatness to one's contemporaries, but not to history.

Greatness is neither chance nor destiny. It is "a compound product in which the genius of the man is one element, and the sphere opened to him by the character of his age and the institutions of his country, is another."

Roosevelt was elected president at the darkest hour of the Great Depression, at a time when the people had lost faith in the ability of their leaders and in the capacity of the free enterprise system to provide the greatest good for the greatest number. He was wise enough to recognize the need for drastic and immediate change, and to perceive that the national mood provided the sphere for it. He initiated the change, gave it direction and impetus, and by so doing irrevocably altered the industrial, economic and sociological philosophy of the nation.

His refusal to imitate, his willingness to improvise and initiate, have surely earned him a dime's worth of recognition by a nation that was founded and developed by men of similar courage and resourcefulness.

A friend has told me that the initials JS, which appear at the base of Roosevelt's shoulder on the dimes, were placed there by a Russian agent in the United States Mint to show his allegiance to Joseph Stalin. Is this true?

As true as the moon is made of Cheddar cheese. The initials are those of John R. Sinnock, who designed the coin, and in the tradition of numismatic sculptors signed the work with his initials. Two years later Sinnock designed the Franklin half dollar and took the precaution of signing it with his full initials, JRS — Stalin's middle name was Vissarionovich.

The appearance of the Kennedy half dollar in 1964 prompted a similar outpouring of hysterical patriotism when the ornate "GR" signature of sculptor-designer Gilroy Roberts was interpreted as the Communist hammer and sickle.

Can you explain the contradiction of the Mercury dime bearing both the portrait of a pagan god and a motto stating a national trust in the Christian God?

There is no contradiction. "Mercury dime" is a misnomer, for the ancient god Mercury is not depicted on the coin. Designer Adolph Weinman created a representation of Liberty, as the coinage law required, and placed wings on the Liberty Cap to symbolize freedom of thought.

What is the meaning of the word "dime?"

"Dime" is derived from the Latin "decima," meaning "tenth part." The coin was originally authorized as a "disme," which the Law of April 2, 1792 defined as the "tenth part of a dollar."

During the years 1837-1964 when the dime contained 90 per cent silver, what was the other 10 percent?

Copper, to increase the hardness, and therefore the wearing qualities, of the largely silver coin.

An eagle appeared on the reverse of all dimes until 1837, when it was replaced by a wreath. Was the change the decision of Christian Gobrecht, the designer of the Liberty Seated dime?

The first coinage act (April 2, 1792) made a representation of an eagle a mandatory device for the reverse of all gold and silver coins. An act of January 18, 1837, eliminated that requirement for the silver dime and half dime.

Is it true, as I've been told, that all 1923-D and 1930-D dimes are counter-feit?

Officially, the Denver Mint did not strike a dime coinage in either 1923 or 1930. For whatever rumor is worth, dimes of either year bearing the Denver "D" mint mark are either of European origin, or were made with official dies and equipment, but without authorization. In either event, they are not official issues.

In the exhibit area of a coin convention, I saw an 1859 Liberty Seated dime that didn't have anything on it to tell that the United States Mint made it. How could this happen?

When the Liberty Seated dime first appeared in 1837, the obverse design included but the figure of Liberty seated and the date. Neither stars nor a legend of national identity were included. UNITED STATES OF AMERICA appeared as part of the reverse design. In 1838, stars were added to the obverse, but the national identification remained on the reverse until 1860, when UNITED STATES OF AMERICA was transferred from the reverse to the obverse, displacing the stars. The change provided an opportunity for the striking of "transitional pattern" dimes using the 1859 obverse die and the 1860 reverse die, neither of which included a legend of national identity. "Transitional pattern" half dimes of the same type and origin were also struck in very limited numbers. Numismatists believe that the mint director deliberately caused these "nationless coins" to be created for sale to collectors.

Why did the San Francisco Mint ever bother to strike a mere 24 dimes in 1894?

The reason isn't known with certainty. A 1905 explanation, attributed to the Mint, maintains that they were struck at the end of the fiscal year when it was discovered that $2.40 in struck coins was needed to balance the books of the branch mint. Another opinion holds that the 24 dimes were struck arbitrarily by the Mint superintendent to give to friends. Only ten of the 1894-S dimes are known to exist. One example sold for $145,000 in 1980, a less well preserved specimen for $50,600 in 1985; the average specimen is probably worth in excess of $100,000.

What United States coinage tradition came to an end with the appearance of the Mercury or Winged Liberty Head dime in 1916?

From the inception of United States regular-issue coinage, the dime had always carried the same obverse device as the higher fractional silver denominations. That tradition ended dramatically in 1916 with the introduction of A.A. Weinman's Winged Liberty Head dime and Liberty Walking half dollar, and H.A. MacNeil's Standing Liberty quarter dollar.

Is there any symbolic significance in the bundle of sticks appearing on the reverse of the Winged Liberty Head dime?

Weinman intended the "bundle of sticks," a fasces enfolding a battle-axe and entwined by an olive branch, to symbolize unity (bound fasces), preparedness (battle-axe) and love of peace (olive branch).

What is the difference between a half dime and a nickel?

The principal difference is one of metallic content. Half dimes were made of .8924 fine silver from 1794 into 1837, and of .900 fine silver thereafter until the denomination was discontinued in 1873. Nickels are made of an alloy of 75 per cent copper and 25 per cent nickel. The nickel was made substantially larger (21.2mm) than the half dime (15.5mm diameter 1829-1873).

I have an 1872 half dime that doesn't carry the mottoes IN GOD WE TRUST and E PLURIBUS UNUM. Is this true of all types of the half dime?

IN GOD WE TRUST never appeared on a half dime of any type. E PLURIBUS UNUM can be found on the Draped Bust-Heraldic Eagle type of 1800-1805, and on the Liberty Cap type of 1829-1837.

Can you tell me how many basic types of dimes there are, and the years they were minted?

Draped Bust (Small Eagle)	1796-1797
Draped Bust (Heraldic Eagle)	1798-1807
Liberty Cap	1809-1837
Liberty Seated (No Stars on Obverse)	1837-1838
Liberty Seated (Stars on Obverse)	1838-1860
Liberty Seated (Arrows at Date)	1853-1855
Liberty Seated (Legend on Obverse)	1860-1891
Liberty Head (Barber)	1892-1916
Liberty Head (Mercury)	1916-1945
Roosevelt (Silver)	1946-1964
Roosevelt (Clad)	1965 to Date

Quarters from 1838

I have noticed that some 1853 quarters are different from all other Liberty Seated type quarters, in that they have arrows at the date on the obverse and rays radiating around the eagle on the reverse. This makes a very attractive design. Why was it not continued?

The arrows and rays were added to the design of the quarter in 1853 to denote a decrease in the weight of the quarter from 103.5 grains to 96 grains. The rays remained on the coin only for 1853, but the arrows through 1855. The arrows, but not the rays, were again employed in 1873-74 to denote a weight increase to 96.45 grains.

I have a 1917 quarter which does not have any stars below the eagle, and all of the other Liberty Standing quarters in my collection have three stars below the eagle. Is this a pattern coin?

No, more than 12 million coins of this type you describe were minted in 1916 and 1917. The design of the initial Standing Liberty quarter portrayed Liberty with a partially unclad bust (which offended Puritanical art critics), and there were no stars beneath the eagle in full flight on the reverse. The design was changed in 1917 to still the criticism. Liberty's torso was covered with a mail corselet; the reverse eagle was raised, and three stars added in the field beneath it. The change produced varieties 1 and 2 of the 1917 quarter. A third variety was created in 1925 when the date area, which had been subject to rapid wear, was recessed to permit higher relief for the numerals and afford it greater protection.

What were the forces which deemed it proper that Washington be featured on the new quarter introduced in 1932, when in his lifetime Washington rejected the idea of having his image featured on a coin?

It isn't unusual for posterity to ignore a man's preference when they design to honor him. Confucius was a teacher who professed no knowledge of a god or hereafter; his disciples reacted to his death by making his teachings a religion, and him a god.

A precedent for a numismatic commemoration of the 200th anniversary of Washington's birth existed in the Lincoln cent, which had been introduced in 1909 to observe the 100th anniversary of Lincoln's birth. The Washington quarter was intended to be a one-year commemorative issue, but it proved so popular with the public that it was continued as a regular issue in 1934.

How many commemorative quarters have been issued by the United States Mint?

Three. The first, the 1893 Isabella quarter, was struck for sale by the Lady Board of Managers of the 1892-1893 Columbian Exposition. This was the only commemorative quarter to be issued by the United States Mint until the Washington Head quarter was issued in 1932 to commemorate the 200th anniversary of the birth of George Washington. It proved to be so popular with the public that it reappeared in 1934 as a regular-issue coin. The third commemorative quarter is the Washington Head Bicentennial quarter featuring the "Drummer Boy" reverse designed by Jack L. Ahr. It was struck in 1975 and 1976 with the dual date 1776-1976.

Who was the model for the Standing Liberty of Hermon MacNeil's beautiful quarter?

MacNeil acknowledged that his rendition of a standing or striding armed Liberty was inspired by Roty's sowing Marianne of the French silver coinage. The actual model was 22-year-old Miss Dora Doscher (later Mrs. H.W. Baum), who also posed for New York City's Pulitzer Memorial Fountain and the famous "Diana" that reposes in the Metropolitan Museum of Art, both figures by Karl Bitter.

Is it true that the Standing Liberty quarters struck from 1917 through 1930 are illegal, or were illegally struck?

That could be said. The legislation that authorized changes in the Variety I Standing Liberty quarter specified that "no change shall be made in the emblems and devices used," and provided only that "the modifications shall consist of the changing of the position of the eagle, the rearrangement of the stars and lettering and a slight concavity given to the surface." Nevertheless, when Variety II appeared in 1917, it was immediately obvious that substantial and unauthorized, and therefore illegal, changes had been made in the "emblems and devices" of the obverse, including the "dressing" of Liberty's breast with "chain mail."

What was the reason for the introduction of a new type quarter dollar, the Seated Liberty, in 1837 after minting of the previous Capped Bust type had already begun?

The Law of January 18, 1837, reduced the weight of the quarter from 6.74 grams to 6.68 grams and increased the fineness from .8924 to .900. The metallic content of a coin was of paramount importance during the era of bullion coinage. A new type quarter facilitated identification of those struck to the revised standard.

What unusual and seldom noticed innovation did Barber introduce to the coinage of the United States with the appearance of his quarter and half dollar in 1892?

The stars on the obverse of both coins are six-pointed, while those on the reverses are the first five-pointed stars to appear on United States coins.

When did the motto IN GOD WE TRUST first appear on the quarter dollar?

The motto was added to the reverse side, displayed on a banner above the eagle, of the Liberty Seated quarter in 1866. It has been retained on quarters since that time.

Is it true that one of the current regular-issue coins of the United States has also served as a commemorative coin?

The Washington quarter dollar was first issued in 1932 to commemorate the 200th birthday of George Washington. It was continued in 1934 (no quarters were struck in 1933) as a regular-issue coin. It became a Bicentennial commemorative in 1976 with the addition of the "Drummer Boy" reverse by Jack L. Ahr. In 1977 it again reverted to regular-issue status with the normal eagle reverse. The Kennedy half dollar and the Eisenhower dollar have also served as both regular-issue and commemorative coins.

Copper-nickel clad coins were introduced in 1965. What was the first denomination to be struck in this new coinage material?

The Washington quarter was the first clad coin to be placed in production (Aug. 23, 1965) and the first clad coin to be released to circulation (Nov. 1, 1965).

Which of the branch mints was the first to strike quarter dollars?

The New Orleans Mint began striking Liberty Seated quarter dollars in 1840. The San Francisco Mint followed in 1855.

Can you tell me how many basic types of quarter dollars there are, and the years they were minted?

Draped Bust (Small Eagle)	1796
Draped Bust (Heraldic Eagle)	1804-1807
Liberty Cap (With motto)	1815-1828
Liberty Cap (Without motto)	1831-1838
Liberty Seated (Without Motto)	1838-1866
Liberty Seated (Arrows and Rays)	1853
Liberty Seated (Arrows, Without Rays)	1854-1855
Liberty Seated (With Motto)	1866-1891
Liberty Head (Barber)	1892-1916
Liberty Standing (No Stars Under Eagle)	1916-1917
Liberty Standing (Stars Under Eagle)	1917-1930
Washington Head (Silver)	1932-1964
Washington Head (Clad)	1965-1974, 1977 to Date
Washington Head (Bicentennial Reverse Cop-Nic Clad & Silver Clad)	Dated 1776-1976

Half Dollars from 1839

Why were the arrows placed at the dates on certain issues of Liberty Seated halves?

In 1853 arrows were placed at the date, and rays on the reverse, to denote a decrease in weight from 206.25 to 192 grains. The rays remained on the coin through 1853, and the arrows through 1855, Arrows, but no rays, were returned to the halves in 1873-74 to denote a weight increase to 192.9 grains.

Is there any explanation why the New Orleans half dollar of 1861 is not worth more than its present valuation, when the U.S. Mint report officially shows that only 330,000 were struck? Other coins of the period with similar mintages are valued much higher.

Another 1,240,000 1861-O half dollars were struck for the government of Louisiana after it seceded from the Union, and 962,633 for the Confederacy. These were struck from the regular U.S. dies, and cannot be distinguished from the U.S. issue.

Through the years I've set aside a lot of 1964 Kennedy halves, every one I've come across, as I once read that they were quite valuable. Can you tell me how much my coins are worth?

Your coins are probably not particularly valuable, in fact they are probably worth less than any of the predecessor Franklin type halves which you could have been putting away to somewhat greater advantage during this time. In 1964 more than 277 million halves were struck at Philadelphia and 156 million at Denver, a figure which more than quadruples the previous high coinage total for a given year.

Although uncirculated (and circulated examples for that matter) 1964 Kennedy halves have been highly cherished as keepsakes, and were long regarded as the most respected tip an American traveling overseas could extend, the coin's current market value is tied to fluctuations in the silver bullion market, as this was the last of the 90-percent silver content halves. The proof edition (3,950,762 specimens struck) does command a significant premium over the premiums realized by other proof edition dates which immediately followed.

I have often heard that the Franklin half carried the advertising of a private firm, but I have never been able to locate such an item. Can you explain where it is located, and how it is possible for this to be?

The words "Pass and Stow, Philada., MDCCLIII," which are inscribed on the Liberty Bell immediately above the upper terminus of the crack, "advertise" the name of the firm that recast the bell after it cracked while being tested for tone, and the year (1753) it was recast. The Philadelphia Assembly ordered the inscription as a courtesy to Pass and Stow.

Fortunately, the nation was made of sterner stuff than its celebrated bell. The first bell cracked upon being tested; the second was defective; the third announced the signing of the Declaration of Independence, but cracked as it was being tolled for the death of Chief Justice John Marshall, in 1835.

A friend told me the slight bulge along the line of Kennedy's neck on the half dollar is intended to represent the point at which the bullet from the assassin's rifle hit our late President? Is that true.

Absolutely not. On many specimens of the coin the feature you are calling attention to, which appears on the truncation of the bust just above the word "We" in the legend, appears quite indistinct. It represents, however, the stylized initials of the coin's designer Gilroy Roberts, then chief sculptor-engraver at the U.S. Mint in Philadelphia.

I'd like to add a 1970 half dollar to my collection, but I don't want to pay the price dealers are asking for the uncirculated and proof versions. Why don't they offer circulated specimens of this issue?

This is a coin that was never released to the public, so any specimen not of uncirculated or better quality would be a mishandled collector coin or one which was accidentally placed in circulation. Actually, in this particular case, a collector encountering a circulated specimen of this coin would have himself a truly rare coin, although its value would certainly be less than that of a good uncirculated or proof specimen.

Only 2.15 million regular-issue half dollars were struck in 1970. They were struck at the Denver Mint to provide a half dollar coin for inclusion in Mint Sets of uncirculated coins sold to collectors. None of the 1970-D half dollars were released to circulation because of the inability to maintain a half dollar containing 40 per cent silver in circulation. Production of a circulation half dollar was suspended until enactment of the Law of December 31, 1970, which authorized production of a cupro-nickel half dollar.

These "D" mint halves command a sizable premium. The proof halves minted at San Francisco that year (2,632,810) also command a substantial premium. All subsequent half dollar issues bear nominal premium values.

The Liberty Head appearing on the obverse of the 1892-1915 Barber half dollar has a familiar look. Has it been employed elsewhere?

Charles E. Barber modeled the handsome Liberty Head of his half dollar, quarter dollar and dime after the Liberty Head appearing on the silver Second Coinage of the 1848-1852 French Second Republic.

Where is the mint mark located on the 1916 Walking Liberty half dollars?

The mint mark of Branch Mint issues of the 1916 half dollars and part of their 1917 issues is located on the obverse immediately below the motto IN GOD WE TRUST. This marked the first appearance of an obverse mint mark on the half dollar since the 1838-O Liberty Cap half dollar carried the "O" mint mark of the New Orleans branch mint immediately above the date. In 1968, the Kennedy half dollar became the third coin of that denomination to bear a mint mark on its obverse.

I enjoy using my coins as conversation pieces when I entertain guests. Is there anything interesting I can say about the rather common Kennedy half dollar?

Few modern coins are more suited to your purpose. Only 24 days elapsed between the time President Johnson asked Congress to authorize the striking of Kennedy half dollars and the first dies were completed at the Philadelphia Mint for proof coinage production. Two skilled Mint engravers collaborated to design the Kennedy half dollar, neither of whom had time to create an original design for his side of the coin. Chief Engraver Gilroy Roberts modeled his likeness of Kennedy after that of the Treasury Department Presidential Medal. Assistant Engraver Frank Gasparro for the reverse of the coin the Presidential Seal adapted the rendering that had been featured on the Kennedy issue in the Treasury's U.S. Presidents medal series.

The Kennedy half dollar bears the initials of two engravers, Gilroy Roberts and Frank Gasparro. The stylized GR monogram signature of Gilroy Roberts is one of but three artistic monograms used by designers of U.S. coins. Gasparro's credit on this half dollar marked the second time he shared his signature on the same coin with another designer. He became the first to do so in 1959 when he designed the Memorial reverse for Victor D Brenner's Lincoln cent.

Although it is a recent addition to the nearly two century old regular-issue coinage of the United States, the Kennedy half dollar has already served as a commemorative coin, with a Bicentennial-theme Independence Hall reverse created by Seth Huntington. Thus far, the Kennedy half dollar has been issued in three metallic varieties — .900 fine silver in 1964, .400 clad silver from 1965 through 1970, plus some of the 1976 Bicentennial strikes, and cupro-nickel clad copper since 1971 — and with mint mark on both the reverse (1964) and the obverse (from 1968). More examples of the Kennedy half dollar were produced during the first eight years of its existence than the total combined production of half dollars during the previous 170 years.

Can you tell me what the small eagle is doing on the reverse of the Franklin half dollar? It looks like an afterthought.

It was an afterthought, one intended to make the coin legal. Chief Mint Engraver John R. Sinnock prepared the design for the Franklin half dollar during World War II. His reverse design, being a copy of the reverse of the Sesquicentennial of American Independence commemorative half dollar he had executed in 1926, did not include an eagle. Sinnock died before the dies were engraved for striking the Franklin half dollar. After his death, Mint officials had second thoughts about the wisdom of ignoring a provision of the law of 1873 which proscribed that the figure of an eagle appear on the reverse of all silver coins above the denomination of 10 cents, a requirement that has been embodied in every primary coinage law enacted since the first of 1792. At their direction, Sinnock's successor, Gilroy Roberts, added the small eagle to the right of the Liberty Bell. That satisfied the law but not the Commission of Fine Arts, which criticized the eagle as "insignificant and hardly discernible."

I have a 1941 proof set on which the designer's initials (AW) are missing from their usual place on the reverse of the half dollar. I have never seen another set like this, and am wondering if it is unique?

A substantial number of the 1941 proof sets were minted with this error, which probably resulted from the accidental removal of the initials lightly incused in the surface of the coin, they are raised on the surface of the die when the dies were being polished.

Has anyone who wasn't a President ever had his picture on a U.S. coin?

Many non-Presidents have appeared on the commemorative coinage of the United States. Franklin is the only non-President to have his portrait on a regular-issue coin, the Franklin 1948-1963 silver half dollar. Incidentally, the appearance of the Franklin half dollar marked the third time that a likeness modeled after a bust by Houdon appeared on a regular-issue coin of the United States.

Why are there so many varieties of halves listed in catalogs for the years from 1805 to 1836?

The basic reason there are so many varieties of halves through those years is that the half dollar was the highest denomination silver coin in production at the Philadelphia Mint. Halves were produced in relatively large numbers, for the period, requiring large numbers of dies, which were individually hand engraved.

The reason halves were produced in large numbers through that 30 year period is that President Jefferson had suspended the minting of silver dollars in 1804. That step was taken because the newly minted coins, which were heavier in weight than the worn Spanish milled dollars alongside which they circulated on a par value basis, tended to flow out of the country to cover the purchase of imported goods, or were melted down for bullion.

With the absence of silver dollars for use in large transactions — $10 gold pieces were also discontinued from 1804 to 1838; although half eagles remained in production throughout the period, quarter eagles were minted only sporadically in very small quantities — half dollars became the desirable coin for the settlement of large transactions, bank reserves and foreign payments. As the halves seldom circulated in the traditional sense, but were principally transferred bank to bank, they survived in relatively large quantities in better than average condition for coins of the period.

Can you tell me how many basic types of half dollar there are, and the years they were minted?

Flowing Hair	1794-1795
Draped Bust (Small Eagle)	1796-1797
Draped Bust (Heraldic Eagle)	1801-1807
Liberty Cap (With Motto, 50 C.)	1807-1836
Liberty Cap (With Motto, 50 CENTS)	1836-1837
Liberty Cap (With Motto, HALF DOL.)	1838-1839
Liberty Seated (Without Motto)	1839-1866
Liberty Seated (Arrows and Rays)	1853
Liberty Seated (With Arrows)	1854-1855
Liberty Seated (With Motto)	1866-1891
Liberty Head (Barber)	1892-1915
Walking Liberty	1916-1947
Franklin Head	1948-1963
Kennedy Head (.900 Silver)	1964
Kennedy Head (.400 Silver)	1965-1970
Kennedy Head (Cop-Nic Clad)	1971-1974, 1977 to Date
Kennedy Head (Bicentennial Reverse Cop-Nic Clad & Silver Clad)	Dated 1776-1976

Silver Dollars

Why is there such a multitude of varieties in the U.S. silver dollar series from 1794-1803?

During the 1790s and the early 1800s, U.S. coinage dies for all denominations were individually hand engraved, with the inevitable result that no two dies of any design type were alike. The difficulty of striking the large coin resulted in excessive die wear and breakage. During this period, the dollar was the only silver coin minted in appreciable quantities. Hand-crafted dies of a short working life, coupled with emphasis on dollar production could only translate into infinite die varieties.

What is the real story behind "The King of American Coins" — the silver dollars of 1804?

This "King of American Coins," this prestigious imposter, is known to exist in fifteen examples, not a one of which was struck in 1804.

The fifteen known examples are segregated into three classes. Eight so-called "originals" form the first class. The other two classes are comprised of so-called "restrikes": a single class two specimen struck over an 1857 Swiss Shooting Thaler; and having a plain edge; and six in class three struck on regular planchets. Their common bond is that all are imposters, and their combined value is estimated at more than four million dollars.

The originals were created in 1834-35 when the secretary of state ordered two complete sets of the nation's coinage for presentation to the King of Siam and the Imaum of Muscat. At the time, the silver dollar was not in production, minting of it having been suspended in 1804, so 1804 was chosen as the last date of production mintage. Unfortunately for the reasoning, the previous dollars struck in 1804 had apparently all been minted with 1803 dies.

It is believed that the restrikes were created clandestinely in 1858 for the

King of American Coins also demands kingly prices. In 1985, one specimen sold for $308,000.

personal profit of Mint employees, but due to a Mint scandal were concealed until 1869.

It has been said, "The King of American Coins' is an impostor, but it was made for a King." That is particularly true today, for only a king can afford one.

Are the Gobrecht silver dollars of 1836-1839 considered to be regular issues?

The famed Gobrecht dollars were prepared in anticipation of a reduction in standard of the silver dollar that would permit issuing of the denomination for the first time since 1804. In view of the fact that the majority of Gobrecht dollars are dated 1836 and the law reducing the weight of the silver dollar wasn't enacted until January 18, 1837, numismatic authorities consider the coins to be pattern dollars. The government, however, lists them as regular issues, and the condition of many of the specimens that have survived is consistent with the belief that they served as a circulating medium of exchange.

Why was the coinage of silver dollars suspended from 1804 through 1839?

Speculators, upon learning that in the West Indies the U.S. dollar was accepted at par with the heavier Spanish dollar, shipped the U.S. dollars to the Indies to be exchanged for their heavier counterpart. The Spanish dollars were then turned into the Philadelphia Mint as bullion to be recoined into a greater quantity of the lighter U.S. dollar. This abuse prevented the U.S. dollars from circulating, and caused President Jefferson to suspend minting of the coin in 1804, although he had no constitutional authority to do so.

I understand some of the silver dollars of 1878 have eight tail feathers on the eagle, while all subsequent Morgan dollars have only seven. Why was this change made?

The eight-feather type was made in error, as Morgan's original patterns had seven. To correct this deviation from the approved design, it was necessary to make a new master die with seven feathers. At least one of the working dies which had been made with the eight-feather master die was directly altered by the engraver's hand, thus creating a 7 over 8 tail feathers variety.

Is it possible to account for the fact that the 1895 Philadelphia silver dollar is available only in proof, when the mint report shows that 12,000 production pieces were struck?

The Morgan dollar was coined in amounts fantastically in excess of circulation requirements. Many issues were simply stored in Treasury vaults to be released in later years. Other supposedly scarce issues (1898-0, 1903-0, 1904-0) suddenly appeared in quantity when they were released to banks to satisfy a former demand for shiny new dollars to be given to children on Christmas. Many supposed that the 1895 dollars were also tucked away in the Treasury awaiting an opportune moment for release. Others believed that they had been melted and recoined under the provisions of the 1918 Pittman Act. Now that the reserve of Treasury-held dollars has been dispersed, the melting theory is generally accepted.

Why was there a suspension of silver dollar coinage from 1905 through 1920?

Coinage of silver dollars was suspended in 1904 because the supply of bullion for its minting, which was supplied under the provisions of the Sherman Act and war revenue bill, was exhausted. Coining of the dollar was resumed in 1921 under the provisions of the Pittman Act of 1918.

I have been told that the Peace Dollar represents the first instance where the word "Peace" was used on a coin of any nation. Could this possibly be true?

Yes, unfortunately. But it is not a commemorative coin, and celebrates a return of peace, rather than the universal ideal of peace.

In 1920 the American Numismatic Association proposed a coin of peace-motif design to commemorative the cessation of hostilities between the Imperial German Government and the people of the United States. Although an enabling resolution for this purpose was allowed to die in Congress without coming to a vote, the peace motif was adopted for the silver dollar under the terms of the Act of 1890, which permits design change without Congressional approval in the instance of a coin that has been minted for twenty-five years.

Is there more than one variety of the Peace dollar?

There are two major varieties of this coin. The 1921 dollars were struck with concave fields and high relief on head and eagle. The 1922-35 dollars were struck with flat fields and low relief. The high relief coins have eight rays below the eagle's tail and four below the N of ONE. The low relief coins have six rays below the tail (seven have been reported on some of the later dates), and three below the N.

I have a silver dollar on which there is a mistake in the lettering. It is a 1922 Peace dollar, and I have noticed that "Trust" in the motto "In God We Trust" is misspelled TRVST. How much is such an error worth?

The spelling of "Trust" TRVST is not an error. It is so spelled on all Peace dollars, on the Liberty Standing quarter dollars, and the substitution of V for U has been extensively employed in the inscriptions appearing on public buildings and monuments.

The immediate precedent will be found in Old English, where the letters U and V were used interchangeably until the 15th to 17th centuries, the latter being used as the printed form, and the former as the cursive or written form wherein the letters of a word are joined. The distant precedent will be found in Latin, where V was first used as a vowel interchangeable with U, and only later as a consonant.

Was the minting of silver dollars suspended from 1928 until 1934 because the Treasury was overstocked with them?

Overstocking of unnecessary silver dollars was a normal condition during the reign of the powerful Silver Lobby. The Pittman Act, which authorized the melting of reserve silver dollars and sale of the bullion to Britian, also provided that the dollars so disposed of be replaced with dollars coined from newly purchased silver. This stipulation was satisfied in April of 1928, and minting of the dollar ceased. The 1934 and 1935 coinages were carried out under an executive proclamation.

Why is it that no silver dollars were coined for circulation after 1935?

Throughout its long and vexatious history, the U.S. silver dollar was never essential to the welfare of the domestic marketplace. In our nation's early days it was principally utilized to ship abroad in quantity to pay for imports. In the latter part of the 19th and early part of the 20th centuries it served chiefly as a subsidy for the Western silver mines. In more recent times it was justified solely by the redemption pledge of silver certificates which stated, "... there has been deposited in the Treasury ... One Silver Dollar payable to the bearer on demand." When that obligation was changed after 1935 to read" ... One Dollar in silver payable to the bearer on demand," that need vanished, for thereafter (until 1967 when the tie between silver and our circulating currency was completely severed) silver bullion on deposit was sufficient backing.

Until the mid-1960s I was always been able to obtain silver dollars from any local bank to give out as birthday gifts, etc., but they never seem to have any now. What happened to the onetime plentiful supply of these?

An upsurge of interest in silver dollars stemming from the belief that no more of them would be coined, and the awareness (caused by the release in 1962 of some supposedly rare issues) that uncirculated dollars of desirable dates were available, resulted in a raid on bank supplies, and the "Great Treasury Raid of 1964" which depleted Treasury stocks by twenty-five million coins. At that point the Treasury suspended distribution of the remainder to formulate a plan for selling them at a premium.

Is it true that the silver dollars of 1794 and part of those struck in 1795 comprise an unauthorized issue?

Technically, yes. The standard for the first U.S. silver dollar, as determined by an analysis of Spanish dollars culled from circulation, proved deficient to the Spanish dollar in weight and fineness. Acting on his own, but in anticipation of passage of remedial legislation before Congress, Director of the Mint David Rittenhouse increased the silver content of the dollar, and struck 1,758 1794 dollars and 203,033 in 1795 to this illegal standard.

Why was the decision made to strike the Eisenhower dollar in two metallic varieties?

The decision was a compromise to end an eighteen-month stalemate between the pro-silver Senate and the anti-silver House of Representatives. The compromise bill authorized a clad cupronickel dollar for general circulation and a limited collector issue of 150 million .400 fine silver pieces to be offered in uncirculated and proof specimens at $3 and $10 respectively.

Is it true that the dollar coin was resurrected after the death of President Eisenhower specifically to provide a medium for an Eisenhower commemorative?

At the time of Eisenhower's death, a "non-silver dollar" for commerce had already been proposed. The timing of the two proposals was certainly a convenience, in that it enabled the Congress to avoid the usual controversary that arises when a change of coinage design is suggested and to circumvent the government's opposition to a commemorative coinage.

I recently read that the Eisenhower dollar was intended to be a quarter. Is this true?

There were a number of proposals for a numismatic recognition of the life and achievement of General-President Eisenhower. Congressman William J. Scherle of Iowa introduced a proposal calling for an Eisenhower quarter dollar on March 31, 1969, three days after Eisenhower's death. In the following weeks there were other proposals, including one for a one-dollar Eisenhower note.

I have heard that Peace dollars were minted in 1964. What's the story?

On August 3, 1964, President Johnson authorized the minting of 45 million .900 fine silver Peace dollars. At some point during the first half of 1965, 30 trial pieces, 76 die adjustment coins and 316,000 1964-D dollars were struck of Peace dollar design. Congressional criticism and a general lack of enthusiasm within the Treasury Department for the striking of silver dollars caused the minting order to be rescinded on May 25, 1965. Mint officials maintain that all of the struck coins were subsequently melted and the dies destroyed. Skeptical numismatic authorities maintain that at least seven of the 1964-dated Peace dollars escaped the melting pot, but that allegation remains to be verified.

A collector friend maintains that the reason no silver dollars were coined from 1874 through 1877 was the new mint law of 1873 did not make a provision for the coining of a silver dollar. This does not seem reasonable to me, so I would like to have your opinion.

Your friend knows the coinage laws. The clumsy and involved revision of coinage laws known as the "Crime of '73" dropped the regular-issue silver dollar entirely, in effect placing the country on a gold standard. The same law authorized the minting of a heavier trade dollar.

What is the difference between a standard silver dollar and a trade dollar, and what was the purpose for which the trade dollar was intended?

Aside from the obvious difference in design, the trade dollar contained 420 grains of .900 fine silver, which was 7½ grains more than the 412½ authorized for the regular-issue dollar. This heavy dollar was issued for the benefit of importers dealing with merchants in China, and was intended to compete in the Orient with the favored Mexican silver dollar, which the lighter regular-issue U.S. dollar had been unable to do.

Why am I having so much trouble locating 1973 Eisenhower dollars for the sets I am putting together for my grandsons? Several banks have allowed me to look through all of the dollars they have on hand, and I find a lot of 1971s and 1972s, some 1974s, but so far no 1973s.

If you want to put together complete date sets of Ike dollars, chances are you'll have to pay substantial premiums for the 1973 coins. In that year the U.S. Mint found that the nearly 285 million dollar coins it had produced the previous two years had pretty much filled the coffers of the nation's banking system, and there just wasn't sufficient demand to merit the production of sizeable quantities of the 1973 issue for circulation issue.

As officials had accepted orders, however, for approximately two million uncirculated mint sets containing six coins each from the Philadelphia and Denver mints, it was necessary to produce a commensurate number of dollar coins at each of the facilities for inclusion in the sets. Both coins command substantial premiums on the collector market, as does the clad metal proof coin of that year (mintage 2,760,339) and the uncirculated silver version (mintage 1,883,140). King of the Ikes, however, is the 1973 silver proof (mintage only 1,013,646) which trades for approximately sixty times its face value.

The Law of April 2, 1792, established the dollar as the "unit" of the U.S. decimal system of coinage. What is meant by "unit" in this instance?

In the era of bullion coinages, the "unit" of a nation's coinage system was the standard from which the bullion values and denominational indices of all other coins in the coinage system were calculated.

Where did George Morgan place his initial on the Liberty Head dollar he designed?

In two places, both cleverly concealed. His initial "M" can be found at the tip of the hair scroll on the truncation of the neck, and on reverse inside the left loop of the wreath bow.

Isn't there something unusual about the appearance of IN GOD WE TRUST on Morgan's Liberty Head dollar?

Morgan engraved the motto with Old English or Gothic lettering, the first use of this kind of lettering in United States coin design.

I have been told that the 1885 proof specimen of the United States Trade dollar that sold in 1980 for $110,000 was illegally struck. Could this be so?

The origin of the ten 1884 and five 1885 proof Trade dollars that are known to exist will probably remain one of the mysteries of numismatics. The Mint has no record of proof Trade dollars being struck during those two years. Numismatists believe the valuable rarities to be the result of private enterprise at the Mint. If the latter theory is correct, the coins are illegal.

Is it true that it was once possible to buy silver dollars from the U.S. Mint for less than face value?

Yes. The opportunity was provided by America's only unwanted and unhonored coin — the only coin of the United States ever to be demonetized — the infamous United States Trade dollar.

Anyone who so wished could purchase Trade dollars from the Mint for 378 grains of silver and coining charge. When it was first issued in 1873, a Trade dollar in the United States was worth about $1.05 in gold. During the following three years, the price of silver declined dramatically, making it possible for the holders of bullion to have it coined into Trade dollars at a total cost of less than the face value of the coins. When the legal tender status of the Trade dollar was revoked in 1876, the gold value of the silver it contained had tumbled to 83 cents. There was, of course, a catch to it. When the merchants realized that the banks wouldn't accept Trade dollars for deposit at face value, they began discounting Trade dollars tendered to them for payment of goods by 10 per cent and more.

I have seen U.S. Trade dollars advertised as "free of chop marks," or "three neatly spaced chops on obverse." What is meant by this reference to "chop marks"?

The chop marks frequently found on the obverse and/or reverse of Trade dollars that traveled to the Orient and back were put there by Chinese merchants at a time when a silver dollar was expected to contain a dollar's worth of silver. The chop mark indicated that the merchant identified by the Chinese character stamped on the dollar had tested the coin and found its weight and fineness to be as represented. The mark enabled him to accept the coin without the bother of testing should a future trade transaction return it to him.

Many collectors consider chop-marked Trade dollars to be defaced or damaged, and therefore lowered in value. Others appreciated their historical significance. A device reminiscent of the Britannia of Roman coins struck on American silver and "defaced" by an Oriental moneychanger provides a numismatic combination that span three disparate civilizations.

What distinction did the appearance of the Bicentennial commemorative Eisenhower dollar bring to Frank Gasparro, designer of the regular-issue Eisenhower dollar?

Adoption of the Bicentennial dollar reverse designed by Dennis R. Williams marked the third time Gasparro's signature initials had appeared on a United States coin with those of other designers. The first two instances were the Lincoln Memorial cent, which he shared with Victor D. Brenner, and the Kennedy half dollar, for which Gilroy Roberts designed the obverse.

Can you tell me how many basic types of the traditional silver dollar coin there are and the years they were minted?

Flowing Hair	1794-1795
Draped Bust (Small Eagle)	1795-1798
Draped Bust (Heraldic Eagle)	1798-1803
Gobrecht (Patterns)	1836-1839
Liberty Seated (Without Motto)	1840-1866
Liberty Seated (With Motto)	1866-1873
Trade Dollar	1873-1885
Liberty Head (Morgan)	1878-1921
Liberty Head (Peace)	1921-1935
Eisenhower Head (Cop-Nic Clad)	1971-1974, 1977-1978
Eisenhower Head (.400 Silver for Collectors)	1971-1974, 1977-1978
Eisenhower Head (Bicentennial Reverse Cop-Nic Clad & Silver Clad)	
	Dated 1776-1976

Susan B. Anthony Dollar

What was the first official act in the drive to put Susan B. Anthony on the dollar coin?

House Bill (#12728) calling for the effigy of Susan B. Anthony to be incorporated on the small size dollar coin was passed by a 6-1 vote on July 23, 1978, by the Historic Preservation & Coinage Subcommittee of the House Committee on Banking, Finance & Urban Affairs.

Why did the Mint make the mistake of making the Anthony dollar almost the same size as the quarters?

The principal reasons were economy, and the feeling that the public would not respond to a bulky, cumbersome coin of the old dollar size. They were right about the second reason, but the public rejected the coin anyway, at least in part because it was readily confused with the quarter. A contributing factor may have been the reeded edge, as the quarter is about as much larger than the nickel as the Anthony is larger than the quarter, but with both coins having reeded edges, a lot of Anthony dollars were given out as quarters, so when received in change they usually were returned to the banks, rather than being maintained in circulation.

Didn't the Post Offices and the Army get involved in trying to make the Anthony dollars circulate?

The Post Offices across the country were enlisted, and passed out larger quantities of the coins, but the effort only delayed the inevitable trip back to the bank. The Defense Department tried to force service personnel stationed in Europe to use the coins in place of paper dollars, but the experiment collapsed because in most countries coins are not accepted for general exchange into currencies.

I see references to varieties, identified as Type I and II, Anthony dollars for both 1979 and 1981. What are they?

Left - Type 1 "Blob" discontinued July, 1979. 2nd - Type 2 geometric design introduced July, 1979. 3rd - Type 1 (1981) created with the same master introduced in July, 1979, but now deteriorated. Right - Type 2 (1981) irregular curves design introduced July, 1981.

All six of the proof coins of those years — cent through dollar for both years — have one of two different "S" mint marks. In both cases the mint mark punch broke at mid-year, and a new design was substituted. Also in both cases, the second, or Variety II mint marks have the most value, as all six of these varieties have low mintages of less than one million.

What were the cost comparisons on the manufacture of an Anthony dollar, compared to a paper dollar?

Paper money costs run about 1.8 cents per note, while the Anthony dollars cost three-cents apiece to mint. The savings was to be in the difference in survival rates. A dollar bill averages 18 months before it wears out. A metal coin is considered to have a minimum life of 15 years in circulation, and indefinite life in a bank vault.

Was there a standard number of Anthony dollars in a roll?

There were at least three standards. They included the old 20 dollars to a roll unit used for the Morgan, Peace and Ike Dollars. Another popular unit size was 25 to a roll, and some banks even wrapped them 40 to a roll, just like quarters.

Please explain the difference between "near date" and "far date" 1979-P Anthony dollars.

So far this is the most important variety discovered for the Anthony dollar. The first Philadelphia strikes, and all of those at San Francisco and Denver with 1979 dates have the date well away from the rim. Out of the total 79-P mintage, the Mint estimated that they struck "up to" 160,750,000 dollars with the date closer to the rim, slightly less than half the year's production. The near date variety has been scarce because nearly all of the coins are still buried in the Federal Reserve Bank vaults. To determine which you have, compare your coin with any 79-D or S dollar — "far date" Philadelphia strikes will have similar separation between the date and rim; "near date" strikes will display the date perceptively, closer to the rim, similar to all issues of 1980 and 1981, as the design was used for all subsequent coins.

Commemoratives

What is a commemorative coin?

All coins are commemoratives to the extent that by their existence they affirm and recall the beginning and development of art and metallurgy, the rise of nationalism, the development of monetary theory, etc. Our present regular-issue presidential-theme coinage honors the achievement of past presidents.

However, by definition and practice the official commemorative coins of the United States were issued supplementary to and concurrent with the regular-issue coinage to specifically honor a person, place or event — generally in celebration of an anniversary. They were struck by the United States Mint with authority from Congress, and are legal tender for their face value.

Regrettably (and this caused their suspension in 1954) U.S. commemoratives were commercially — as well as historically — motivated. Rather than being released to general circulation, they were sold to the sponsoring centennial commission at face value, and resold to the public at a premium.

Commemoratives were issued intermittently from 1892 through 1954 in 157 distinct varieties, including mint marks and dates. The total includes forty-eight major types of half dollars, creating one hundred and forty-three varieties, one silver dollar, one quarter dollar, six major types of gold dollars forming nine varieties, two two-and-a-half-dollar gold pieces and two fifty-dollar gold slugs.

Commemorative designs were adapted to our circulation issue quarter, half dollar and dollar coinage in 1976 for the Bicentennial. In 1982-84, following a 28 year lapse, the issue of special issue commemoratives was renewed with the introduction of the single coin George Washington 250th anniversary of birth half, followed a three coin series to commemorate the Summer Olympics in Los Angeles.

I have a rare Columbian half dollar. It was found in my grandfather's estate. How much is it worth?

The Columbian half dollar is historically significant in being the first U.S. commemorative coin, but it is neither rare nor particularly valuable.

It was issued in conjunction with the World's Columbian Exposition in Chicago in 1893, the theme of which was the 400th anniversary of the first voyage of Columbus to the Americas. In lieu of a requested $5,000,000 appropriation to help defray the cost of the Exposition, Congress authorized the striking of 2,500,000 souvenir half dollars from subsidiary silver coin held by the Treasury. They were sold at the Exposition for $1.00 each.

A delay in the opening of the Exposition resulted in two date varieties of the coin, 1892 and 1893. A substantial number of the coins were unsold. The surplus 1893 strikes were melted. The unsold stocks were released into circulation by the Chicago banks holding them as par security against loans. Either date is worth but a few dollars in desirable condition.

Is it true that we issued a silver dollar in honor of Lafayette?

Yes. The commemorative Lafayette silver dollar of 1900 was issued in conjunction with the erection of an equestrian statue of Lafayette in Paris during the Exposition of 1900. Both the statue and the enabling coin were an expression of gratitude for Lafayette's contribution to the rebel cause during the American War for Independence. It is numismatically significant in being the

first U.S. commemorative coin of one-dollar denomination, and the first authorized U.S. coin to bear the portrait of one of our presidents (Washington).

The coin was sold by the Lafayette Memorial Commission for $2.00 each and the profits, augmented by the contributions ($50,000) of American school children, paid for the erection of the statue.

What is the Isabella quarter? How valuable is it?

The Isabella quarter (which bears the portrait of Queen Isabella I of Spain) was the second commemorative coin issued by the United States, and the first and only of 25¢ denomination. (The 1932 Washington-quarter was initially intended to be a commemorative, but was continued as a regular issue in 1934.)

Pressure upon Congress by Susan B. Anthony and the suffrage movement led to a provision for a board of lady managers in the bill for the Columbian Exposition. Part of the money allotted to them to promote their interest in the Exposition was in the form of 40,023 Isabella quarters. They were sold as souvenirs at $1.00 each.

As with the Columbian half, sales were disappointing; 15,809 were subsequently melted.

Specimens are valued at about $500 in typical uncirculated condition.

Does the Pilgrim half dollar commemorate one or two events?

The Pilgrim Tercentenary commemorative half dollar was issued in 1920 to commemorate the 300th anniversary of the landing of the Pilgrims. It was

reissued in 1921 with the addition of the date 1921 in the obverse field. There is an opinion that the 1921-dated commemoratives commemorate the 300th anniversary of the founding of Plymouth, but it is by no means a unanimous one.

Why is a "2x4" sometimes appended to listings of Missouri half dollars?

The reason can be found in your pocketbook. A five-pointed star inserted between a 2 and 4 that appears on the obverse of about a fourth of the Missouri Centennial half dollars was placed there to deliberately create a "variety" to lure the dollar of the collector haunted by the notion that his devotion to the hobby is measured by the completeness of his collection. The device indicated that Missouri is the 24th star on the flag, as do the 24 stars on the reverse of both varieties. In similar instances, a five-pointed star was employed to create a variety of the Grant Centennials, and a 2X2 did as much for the Alabama Centennial.

Why was the star added to the Grant Memorial half dollar?

The 1922 Grant Memorial half dollar commemorates the 100th anniversary of the birth of the Civil War general and two-term president, Ulysses S. Grant. The commission handling the sale of the coins, the profit from which was used to finance various Grant memorial projects, caused the star to be

incused by the Mint on the obverse of a modest percentage of the issue to create duplicate sales to some collectors. This is also true of the Grant Memorial gold dollar. Buyers of this variety should exercise great care for private initiative has been known to add the star outside the Mint.

How scarce is the Hawaiian commemorative half dollar?

On the 150th anniversary of the discovery of the Hawaiian Islands by Captain James Cook, 10,058 (including 50 presentation proofs) commemorative half dollars were issued for the Captain Cook Sesquicentennial Commission, and sold through the Bank of Hawaii. Distribution was equally divided between the continental United States and the islands. The coins were sold at $2.00 each, with a limit of five to a buyer.

The low mintage, even distribution and theme of the commemorative combined to make it a popular coin. It has commanded a substantial premium from its inception, and today has one of the highest catalog values of any commemorative half dollar, regardless of condition.

Is the Arkansas Centennial commemorative coin with the portrait of Joseph Robinson the only United States coin to bear the portrait of a living person?

It is neither the only nor the first. The first living person to be portrayed on a coin of the United States was Governor Thomas E. Kilby of Alabama. His portrait and that of William Bibb, the first governor of Alabama, appeared on the 1921 Alabama Centennial half dollar.

However, the Arkansas coin has other unusual features. Although it bears the date 1936, it was not issued until 1937. The enabling act designated the undated portrait side as the reverse. Collectors were not impressed, and consider the official reverse to be the obverse of the coin.

What commemorative half dollar do you consider to be the most artistic?

"Artistic" is a matter of opinion, not a description. The object called beautiful can be measured, weighed, analyzed and defined; but the quality of beauty is a chimera having neither permanence nor universal validity.

The Oregon Trail commemorative is certainly outstanding in its draftsmanship and symbolism. The obverse of Indian clad in ceremonial bonnet and dignity, standing before a map of the United States with arm outstretched toward the east in the futile posture of primitive defiance, eloquently depicts the age-old conflict between the free nomad and the tinkers and farmers who flowed across the land like a sea of tar, felling the forests and furrowing the plains, rooting more firmly than the oak and pine whose shadow they brush from the hills. On the reverse, a Conestoga wagon rolls irrevocably toward the setting sun, conquering with oxen and wheel, prevailing through numbers.

What details can you provide me on the Booker T. Washington half dollar?

Booker T. Washington is associated with two commemorative half dollars: the Booker T. Washington coin issued from 1946 through 1951, and the Booker T. Washington-George Washington Carver coin issued from 1951 through 1954.

The Booker T. Washington commemorative was the first United States coin to bear the likeness of a black, and the first to be designed by one (Isaac

Scott Hathaway). It was issued to commemorate the black educator's work in behalf of black education and the school at Tuskegee. This theme is augmented on the 1951-54 coin by a concurrent commemoration of Carver's plant experiments and advocacy of diversified farming that revolutionized the agriculture of the post-bellum South.

The intent of the Booker T. Washington Commission was to sell the authorized mintage of five million commemoratives to the nation's fifteen million Negroes at $1.00 each. The plan failed when only 3 percent of the Negro population responded to the project. The excesses of these commemoratives — the multiplicity of date and mint varieties and allegations of financial hanky-panky in their merchandising — were in part the cause of a cessation in commemorative issues which encompassed the next 29 years.

Does the motto "In God We Trust" appear on all of the commemorative coins of the United States?

Nearly all. The motto does not appear on the Isabella quarter dollar, the Columbian and Missouri Centennial half dollars or the Lafayette dollar. It appears on the Philadelphia Sesquicentennial quarter eagle ($2.50) but on no other gold commemorative, other than the two varieties of the Panama-Pacific $50 gold "slug." The Columbian and Missouri Centennial half dollars are the only commemoratives of that denomination to lack all three statutory inscriptions: LIBERTY, E. PLURIBUS UNUM and IN GOD WE TRUST.

When did the practice of issuing commemorative coins begin?

Commemorative coins are nearly as old as coinage, which began about 700 B.C. The first commemorative coin of record was issued by Anaxilas of Rhegium in 480 B.C. to commemorate his chariot victory at the Elis Olympic Games, which he won driving a biga of mules.

Why did the United States wait until 1892, a century after the establishment of the Mint, before issuing its first commemorative coin?

Until 1892 the United States followed the custom inaugurated during the War for Independence of issuing national medals as commemoratives.

Is it true that when the statue of Lincoln in the Lincoln Memorial appeared on the reverse of the cent in 1959, Lincoln became the first person to have his picture on both sides of a U.S. coin?

It is true of regular-issue coinage. A likeness of the Marquis de Lafayette can be found on both sides of the 1900 Lafayette U.S. commemorative silver dollar.

How much money did the Los Angeles Olympics effort receive from the sale of the Olympics commemoratives.

The amount turned over by the Treasury Department was $73.4 million, which was shared equally by the U.S. Olympic Committee and the Los Angeles Organizing Committee. The payments were generated from a $10 premium per coin charged on the sale of each silver dollar, and $50 each on the gold pieces.

How do the quantities of issue for the 1982 George Washington 250th anniversary of birth commemorative half compare with quantities struck of earlier U.S. commemorative coins?

The Washington coin was produced in far greater numbers than any of the earlier commemorative issues. The combined production of uncirculated and proof specimens exceeded 8.45 million pieces; in 1986 nearly 1.5 million unsold specimens were melted. The proof version originally sold for $10 and the uncirculated for $8.50; prices were subsequently increased to $12 and $10 each, respectively.

The 1982 Washington commemorative enjoyed a total sales of 2,210,458 uncirculated and 4,894,044 proof examples. Previously, the 1952 Philadelphia Mint struck version of the Washington-Carver commemorative half dollar coinage had enjoyed the largest sales, with a net issuance of 2,006,292 examples. Only eight other U.S. commemoratives had been issued in quantities of more than 200,000 specimens, the 1892 Columbian (950,000), 1893 Columbian (1,550,405), 1923-S Monroe Doctrine (274,077), 1925 Stone Mountain (1,314,709), 1946 (1,000,546; unknown quantity melted) and 1946-S (500,279) Booker T. Washington, and 1950-S (512,091) and 1951 (510,082) issues of the same series.

Historically, the total coinage of U.S. commemoratives from 1892 through 1954 had numbered approximately 12.28 million pieces, more than 5.5 million of the total having been posted as a result of the 1946 through 1954 production of the Booker T. Washington and Washington-Carver series. Actual sales of the 1982 Washington commemorative (7,104,502 pieces) exceeded the total number of all commemorative issues sold (under 6.8 million) from the 1892 Columbian Exposition offering, the first, through the Iowa Centennial issue of 1946, the last, excepting the Booker T. Washington and Washington-Carver issues.

How many coins must a person acquire to have a complete set of 1983-84 Los Angeles Olympiad commemorative coinage?

A complete type set would consist of just three pieces; silver dollars dated 1983 and 1984, and the 1984 ten dollar gold pieces. A complete set featuring all of the mintmark and striking varieties would consist of 13 coins.

The 1983 and 1984 silver dollars come in four varieties each; uncirculated quality specimens bearing the Philadelphia, Denver and San Francisco mintmarks, plus the "S" mint proof edition, for each year. The gold coin, thus far the only U.S. coin to carry a "W" mintmark, was struck in both uncirculated and proof qualities at the West Point minting facility, and in proof quality at the Philadelphia, Denver and San Francisco mints.

Is the Eisenhower dollar a commemorative?

Technically it is not a commemorative; the enabling act proposed it as a replacement for the suspended Peace dollar.

Semantics aside, the Eisenhower dollar is by the historical significance of its themes a dual commemorative. The obverse bears witness to the nation's appreciation of the contribution of General-President Eisenhower to the national accomplishment. The reverse commemorates the initial moon landing on July 20, 1969.

Other commemoratives that are not — strictly speaking — commemoratives are the Bicentennial dollar, half dollar and quarter, first issued in 1975 in anticipation of the nation's 200th anniversary in 1976. The three coins, with special reverse designs, bear the dual dates 1776-1976. In that respect they are true commemoratives, drastically changed from regular circulation coins. But they were struck for circulation (no single dated dollars, halves or quarters were produced for the years) and the large mintages authorized for each puts them in the realm of everyday circulating coins. Perhaps they should be called "circulating commemoratives."

Gold Coins

I have seen early gold coins that appear to be bigger than gold coins of like denominations of later years. Did they at one time have more gold in them?

The coins of the eighteenth and nineteenth centuries were larger in diameter and thinner than gold coins of later years, although there was not a significantly higher amount of fine gold in these early coins. This was the case with most denominations of silver coins as well.

An exception would be the Type I gold dollar of 1849-54 which was smaller and thicker than subsequent gold dollars.

What is an "Eagle" as the term applies to U.S. coins?

A ten-dollar gold piece. Alexander Hamilton, a strong advocate of decimal-denomination coinage, proposed that 100 units to a dollar and ten dollars to an eagle would enable the average citizen to more easily understand the mathematical structure of the monetary system.

The term was never used on the coin itself to denote its value, but the ten-dollar gold coin has been known as an "Eagle" down through the years. The term has also been applied to the divisions and multiple of the ten-dollar gold piece: quarter eagle for $2.50, half eagle for $5 and double eagle for $20.

What makes the early U.S. gold coins so prohibitively expensive?

Their comparative rarity. When the United States, upon the recommendation of Alexander Hamilton, adopted a bimetallic monetary standard in the ratio of 15 (silver) to 1 (gold), the ratio conformed to that in general world usage. But by 1799 the ratio in European commercial centers had broadened to 15-3/4 to 1, giving our gold coins a higher bullion value than their face value. The undervalued gold coins flowed out of the country, or were melted for bullion. This destruction, coupled with the subdued mintage of the time, necessarily produced the present imbalance of supply and demand, and consequent high prices.

What was the purpose of the $3 gold piece?

It is widely assumed that the $3 gold piece was issued to facilitate the purchase of three-cent stamps by the hundred. The belief is supported by the fact that the silver three-cent piece was issued to make purchase of the stamp less bothersome, and by the discontinuing of the $3 gold piece when the postal rates were changed.

Were one-dollar gold coins ever used, or were they always hoarded?

The fact that so many circulated pieces are available today substantiates that they were actively employed as a medium of exchange. Gold coins were a favorite of the business community because they had an intrinsic worth independent of the ability of a government to support its money.

Three major types of gold dollars minted in the United States were the coronet (1849-54), small Indian head (1854-56) and large Indian head (1856-89).

Is the 1848 gold quarter eagle that has "CAL." punched in the field above the eagle on reverse a private or territorial gold issue?

Although the story of this unusual, and unusually valuable, gold piece is part of the history of the Territory of California, it is an official coin of the United States, struck at the Philadelphia Mint.

California was not yet a state when Military Governor Col. Richard B. Mason collected 230 ounces of California gold and, thinking this tangible evidence of the mineral wealth of the territory would add impetus to the movement for statehood, sent it to Washington by military courier. The courier

carried the gold to Washington by way of Peru, Panama, Jamaica and New Orleans and delivered it to Secretary of War W.L. Marcy. Marcy sent it on to the mint at Philadelphia, suggesting that a portion of it be reserved for medals, and that the balance "be used in striking quarter eagles bearing a distinguishing mark."

Mint Director R. M. Patterson struck 1,389 quarter eagles from the California gold, and to distinguish them from regular issues had CAL. hand-stamped above the eagle. These gold coins that helped bring California into the Union have a distinctive brassy color imparted by the high silver content of California gold.

Why can't a collector own a 1933 $20 gold piece?

None of the 1933 $20 coins were released to general circulation. Almost predictably, a few specimens did escape the melting pot. They are subject to confiscation by the Treasury Department. The last of these coins to be seized was taken from the King Farouk collection when it went on sale in 1955.

Are gold coins held in storage by the Treasury Department?

No. All gold held by the government is in the form of gold bullion.

At a recent coin show I heard the term "St. Gaudens Twenty" used. What was being referred to?

Specifically, a $20 gold coin of the design minted from 1907 to 1933. The expression denotes a deserved recognition of the coin's designer, Augustus Saint-Gaudens. The Saint-Gaudens double eagle is universally acclaimed a masterpiece of the medalist's art; in the words of President Teddy Roosevelt, "more beautiful than any coin since the days of the Greeks."

There are a lot of strange terms used in coin collecting. Among them is "Paquet Reverse". What is this?

The term refers to a special reverse design employed on some 1861 dated $20 gold coins, principally on San Francisco strikes. Comparison with the initial piece of this year will readily reveal that the legends of the Paquet Reverse contain taller and bolder letters. This reverse derives its name from its designer, A. C. Paquet.

Where did the United States Mint obtain gold for coinage before the California gold strike?

Rutherford County, North Carolina, supplied most of the nation's gold from 1790 to 1840.

I have a little gold coin that looks like it was made backwards; it says 2½ dollars on the back. What is it?

Your coin, issued between 1908 and 1929, is a $2.50 gold piece (quarter eagle) issued by the United States Mint. The reason it appears "backwards" is because the design is incused (sunken) rather than bas-relief (raised) from the field as most coins are. The $5 gold coins of this period are of smaller design.

Indian head design was used on obverse of U.S. gold eagles ($10) from 1907 to 1933. Design is by Augustus Saint-Gaudens, who also created the double-eagle of the same period.

Incuse designs (cut into the coin surface, rather than raised) have appeared on only two U.S. coins — the gold quarter eagle (shown) and the half eagle. Both were designed by Bela Lyon Pratt and minted from 1908 through 1929.

Does a gold coin that has been soldered to a chain or one that has a hole in it from having been used on a necklace have a deteriorated value?

Definitely. The state of preservation is a determining factor in arriving at the value of any numismatic item. A piece such as you describe would be considered a jewelry piece, and would generally be considered collectible only if it was a rare type or date of issue.

Why was the Type I gold dollar made larger and thinner in 1854?

A change in material or philosophy is but seldom born of single cause. One of the reasons for enlarging the Type I dollar is that skilled but larcenous hands developed the knack of slicing the thick coin in half, paring a bit of gold from the center, and rejoining the diminished halves with solder.

If the motto E PLURIBUS UNUM was made a mandatory part of coinage design in 1873, where is it on the Saint-Gauden's double eagle?

The Saint-Gauden's double eagle is the only modern coin of the United States to have a lettered eagle. The motto E PLURIBUS UNUM appears on the edge of the coin, with stars between the words.

What is a gold "slug"?

"Slug" is a nickname for a $50 gold coin of both official and private origin, and for bars or ingots of California gold issued in denominations or values of up to $150. The only $50 gold slugs ever coined for the public by the United States government were the Panama-Pacific commemoratives made in 1915 for the Panama-Pacific Exposition which was held to celebrate the completion of the Panama Canal. This commemorative was issued in both round and octagonal shape, as were the earlier private slugs issued in California which inspired this unusual issue.

According to Western legend, the large, heavy gold pieces received the name "slug" from the practice of wrapping them in a bandana and using the impromptu bludgeon to slug unwary miners before relieving them of their gold dust.

Is it true that the "official" U.S. price of gold was once as low as $20 an ounce?

In 1834, Congress set the price of gold in the United States at $20.67 an ounce. This price level remained in effect until January 31, 1934, when gold's price was officially raised to $35 an ounce, a move which had the effect of devaluing the dollar 40.94 per cent. On February 12, 1973 the official U.S. price was raised to $42.22 an ounce, and the dollar devalued 10 per cent. The 1834 Act also fixed the price of silver at $1.2929 an ounce, the price remaining in effect until July 14, 1967, when the Treasury announced that it would no longer engage in the selling of silver at that rate to maintain an artificially low market level.

What is the difference between "karat" and "fineness" as they refer to the purity of gold?

The terms are the jeweler's and the coiner's way of expressing quantitative value. Fineness denotes the number of parts of gold, or the per cent of gold, an alloy contains. A gold item identified as .750 fine contains three parts of gold and one part of another metal, such as copper, and consequently contains 75 per cent pure gold. A karat is defined as "a unit of fineness for gold equal to 1/24 part of pure gold to an alloy." A gold item identified as 18-karat gold contains 75 per cent of pure gold, and consequently has a fineness of .750.

I have a note by means of which Wells Fargo transferred gold from San Francisco to New York. This document is called a "second exchange" note. What does this mean?

Wells Fargo, and other express companies, transferred money from the West to the East by means of first, second and third exchanges. The exchanges traveled by different routes. One went by sea around Cape Horn, another by sea with a land crossing of Panama, and the other overland. The first exchange to arrive at the designation point was honored, whereupon the other two were automatically voided.

The four-dollar gold "stella" bears the motto DEO EST GLORIA. What does this mean?

Had Congress approved of the proposed stella, it would, in effect, have served as an international trade coin. It was thought that the religious motto adopted for use on U.S. coins, IN GOD WE TRUST, the use of which was associated with the Christian deity, would be inappropriate for a coin intended to serve people of all religious faiths. DEO EST GLORIA ("glory to God") was considered to be more readily acceptable to the world community.

I have a 1908 $10 gold piece that has the words "In God We Trust" on the reverse, and my buddy has one that doesn't. Why is this?

When the Saint-Gaudens eagle and double eagle of new design appeared in 1907, it was soon discovered that the religious motto had been omitted from them. It had been removed at the suggestion of President Teddy Roosevelt, who thought that using a coin as an advertising medium for God was sacrilegious. The motto was restored by Act of Congress in 1908, resulting in two varieties of each coin for that year.

Why did President Roosevelt act in 1933 to restrict the ownership of gold by American citizens?

The President moved to require holders of gold to deliver their holdings in the metal, except for coins of numismatic merit, to the government for one purpose and one purpose only: to prevent individuals from profiting by the official revaluation of gold from $20.67 per ounce to $35. Only half of the $571 million worth of gold coin estimated to be held by the public in 1933 was ever turned in.

Can Americans legally own gold coins?

American citizens have never been prohibited from collecting or otherwise owning in any quantity most gold coin issues. However, Treasury regulations invoked under the Gold Reserve Act of 1934 prohibited U.S. citizens from holding gold in other forms than those intended for customary industrial and artistic purposes, plus items deemed to be of sufficient numismatic merit. This included all gold coins dated 1933 or earlier, except the U.S. $20 piece of 1933, plus selected issues of later dates through 1965. This regulation was revised on Dec. 17, 1973, to include all gold coins dated 1959 or earlier, but excluding all issues of subsequent dates. In 1974 Congress acted to authorize unrestricted ownership of gold in all forms as of Dec. 31, so Americans may now legally own any gold coin or other numismatic item.

I have heard it is illegal to own foreign gold coins. Is that correct?

It was illegal to own, buy or sell foreign gold coins dated after 1933 — except for specific exceptions — until Dec. 31, 1974, at which time the Treasury removed all restrictions on the ownership of gold by Americans. Until the ban was lifted, all eligible gold coins which individuals wished to purchase from abroad could not be brought into the country without a special gold import license.

The denomination was indicated as 1/100 and 1/200 on the early copper cents and half cents. Has any other coin of the United States ever had the denomination indicated fractionally?

The denomination of the gold quarter eagle ($2.50) was stated on the coin as 2½ D. or 2½ DOLLARS from 1808 through 1929 on four basic types. The fraction ½ indicated the value on the 1796-1797 Draped Bust-Small Eagle half dollar.

Grant Gold
Dollar without star.

Star added
to obverse design.

Among the coins left in my father's estate is a small gold coin identified simply as a Grant Gold Dollar, and dated 1922. Is it a regular U.S. coin?

It is a commemorative gold coin struck as a centenary souvenir of Ulysses S. Grant's birth. There are two principal varieties, with star and without; the latter is slightly more valuable.

I have read that the unusual four-dollar gold "stella" struck by the United States in 1879 was intended to be a "metric" coin. Can you tell me what is meant by this?

A four-dollar gold coin was envisioned by John A. Kasson, U.S. Minister to Austria, as an international coin approximate in value to the metric-based coins issued by the European members of the Latin Monetary Union, and which were created as a device to standardize coinage systems. A value of four dollars made the stella approximately the equal of the Italian 20 lire, French 20 francs, Austrian and Dutch 8 florins and the Spanish 20 pesetas, all of which were gold coins. Patterns were struck in gold, aluminum, copper and white metal. If adopted for issue, the stella would have been made of "goloid," a combination, with copper, of gold and silver in equal quantities by value, thus serving to reaffirm America's commitment to bimetallism at a time when the major trading nations of Europe were increasingly favoring a gold standard.

What is the gold content of my U.S. gold coins?

All U.S. gold coins struck subsequent to the enactment of the law of Jan. 18, 1837, have had a .900 fine gold content. The weight of the $20 (double eagle) piece is specified at 33.436 grams, resulting in a pure gold content of .96750 ounce. All lower denominations gold coins have a proportional fine gold content. The following table illustrates the value of the gold bullion content in quarter eagles, half eagles, eagles and double eagles at selected incremental bullion market price levels:

Gold Bullion Value	$320	$360	$400	$440	$480	$520	$560	$600
$2.50, Quarter Eagle	38.69	43.53	48.37	53.21	58.04	62.88	67.72	72.55
$5, Half Eagle	77.40	87.07	96.75	106.42	116.10	125.77	135.45	145.12
$10, Eagle	154.80	174.15	193.50	212.85	232.20	251.55	270.90	290.25
$20, Double Eagle	309.60	348.30	387.00	425.70	464.40	503.10	541.80	580.50

Private Gold Coins

What is meant by the term "Private Gold"?

In a simpler time — before the railroads bound the disparate parts of the country into a united whole — much of the country was separated from the financial centers of the East by formidable barriers of distance and primitive transportation. The developing industry and commerce of the remote parts was burdened by a lack of sufficient U.S. coinage. Although no state or territory had the right to coin money, private sources in the gold-mining areas of Georgia, North Carolina, Utah, Colorado, Oregon and California endeavored to fill the need by issuing necessity pieces of various denominations and shapes. These do-it-yourself gold coins struck outside of the U.S. Mint are known as "Private Gold."

What are "California fractional gold pieces"?

California fractional gold pieces are gold coins of small denomination issued by jewelers, engravers and goldsmiths to satisfy a need for small change that developed in California during the gold rush days. These tiny gold pieces were issued in denominations of quarter dollar, half dollar and dollar from 1852 to 1882, in both round and octagonal form. Genuine fractional gold pieces generally have a Liberty Head, Indian Head, or Washington Head on obverse; a wreath, beaded circle or eagle on reverse; and a value designation stated as "Cents," "Dol," "Doll," or "Dollar."

Is there an easy way to tell the difference between a genuine California fractional gold piece and a California token or souvenir?

The genuine piece must bear an actual reference to a denominational value stated as "cents" or a form of "dollar." A law passed in 1882 prohibits the use of the word "dollar" on any gold coin other than issues of the United States Mint. Imitation tokens and souvenirs made after that date and back-dated usually state the value numerically as 1/4, 1/2 or 1 to avoid the legal compli-

Fractional Gold Coin   Souvenir Gold Piece

cations use of any form of the word "dollar" would make them liable to even though the imitation pieces, not being reproductions of government issues, could not legally be considered counterfeits. Many of the tokens made immediately after 1882 are of good gold and weight, but this does not make them genuine fractional pieces. Souvenir issues of recent make are usually made of gold-plated brass.

I recently saw an octagonal Washington Head California gold piece advertised that did not bear the word "dollar" or an abbreviation of it, but did carry the word CHARM. Can such a piece by authentic?

Others have also wondered. Octagonal Washington Head gold pieces containing the proper amount of gold for the 1/2 dollar denomination of California fractional gold are not uncommon. It is believed that such pieces were correctly dated, and in some instances may have circulated as coin. But most authorities believe them to be exactly what the name they bear indicates, a charm.

Who produced the first gold dollar in the United States, the government or a private coiner?

Government issue gold dollars weren't authorized until March 3, 1949. The first gold dollars were produced sometime after 1830 by Christopher Bechtler,

a German metallurgist, and his son August at the private mint they maintained at Rutherfordton, North Carolina. The Bechtlers struck gold coins in three denominations, $1, $2.50 and $5.00, in a great variety of sizes, weights and fineness.

Why was the need for gold coins so urgent in gold-rush California that private minters literally broke the law to provide it while the government obligingly looked the other way?

The discovery of gold at Sutter's Mill caused one of the greatest stampedes in history. Tens of thousands of fortune seekers poured into an area where few had existed before. California was too remote for the U.S. Mint to provide with adequate coinage. Foreign coins passed current everywhere, but there wasn't enough of them. Gold dust and nuggets circulated freely, but the U.S. customs house refused to accept it and badly needed merchandise piled up in government warehouses for want of a medium acceptable for payment of duties. Need and opportunity were sufficient incentives for enterprising individuals to begin minting gold "coins" and ingots.

I understand that private firms issued gold coins in California before the United States did. What firm issued the first such coins, and what face value did they bear?

The first of the California private gold coins are considered to be the half-eagles ($5.00) issued by Norris, Grieg & Norris in 1849. These coins are mentioned in a newspaper account dated May 31, 1849. Gold coins were also issued in California in 1849 by Templeton & Reid, Moffat & Co., Massachusetts & California Co., Miners' Bank, Cincinnati Mining & Trading Co., J.S. Ormsby and the Pacific Co.

I have read that by the end of 1849, there was a "virtual avalanche" of California private gold, mostly larger denominations. Why, then, are these pieces so scarce and prohibitively expensive?

These illegal pieces were produced in great number. The need for them was so pressing that no action was ever brought against any of the coiners. The reason for the large premium these coins command is, of course, that few have survived. The coiners agreed to redeem their issues and to put enough gold in them to assure that intrinsic and face values would be equal. In a few cases, the gold content actually exceeded the face value. Most of the coins were eventually redeemed and melted to recover their gold content.

According to the coin catalogs, the first United States coins weren't struck by a branch mint in California until 1854. What were the fifty-dollar pieces struck in California in 1851 at the United States Assay Office, which was a Provisional Government Mint, if they weren't United States coins?

It is true that in 1851 Augustus Humbert, United States Assayer of gold in California, issued fifty-dollar gold pieces on which he stamped the value, fineness, his name and a government stamp, and that they were accepted as legal tender on a par with U.S. gold coins. They were not, however, recognized at the United States Mint as an official issue of coins, but simply as ingots.

In Western movies I have seen "Forty-Niners" paying for goods with "a pinch of dust." Since the dust was raw or unrefined gold, how could anyone really be sure what a particular miner's "dust" was actually worth?

Miners and shopkeepers quickly learned to judge the approximate value of gold dust by its color, which varied with the amount of silver in combination with the gold. Gold in Sacramento and Stanislaus Counties had an average value of $18.60 an ounce. That found in Mono County had such a heavy silver content that it bore a distinct resemblance to silver in color. It had an average value of $11.35 an ounce. The first attempt to arrive at an average price occurred on September 9, 1848, when the price of California gold was set at $16 an ounce, providing it had "good color."

I am intrigued by the devices employed on the private gold coins of the Mormon Territory. Can you explain what they mean or symbolize?

The two devices most commonly appearing on Mormon gold coins are a beehive and clasped hands. The beehive, a favorite device of the Mormons, related to "State of Deseret," the first name given to the Mormon Territory. "Deseret" means "honey bee." The clasped hands symbolize strength in unity.

Is it true that the gold Beaver coins of Oregon were minted despite the fact that the law authoring them had been declared unconstitutional?

Yes, but all of the private gold coins were illegally issued. The February 16, 1849, law of the Oregon legislature which provided for a mint and authorized the striking of five and ten-dollar coins made of gold without alloy, was passed after Oregon had been brought into the Union as a territory by an act of Congress. When the territorial governor arrived a few weeks later, he declared the Oregon coinage act unconstitutional.

Eight private citizens then formed the Oregon Exchange Company and proceeded to strike gold coins of the denominations and standard proscribed by the outlawed law. In the view of collectors, they did their job too well. When it was discovered that the Oregon gold Beavers contained 8 per cent more gold than necessary, they were bought up and shipped to California to be profitably recoined into $50 gold slugs. Consequently, Oregon gold coins are scarce and expensive today.

Did the California minters of private gold coins cease operating when the United States established a branch mint in the state?

Only a relatively few continued to strike their private issues after 1850. However, Wass, Molitor & Company and Kellog & Company produced a great quantity of coins in denominations of $10, $20 and $50 in 1855, although the San Francisco branch mint was then producing coins.

Is there a record of the largest nugget of gold ever found in California?

We tend to think of a "nugget" of gold being no larger than a walnut, and usually much smaller. Webster, however, defines nugget as "A solid lump, especially a native lump of precious metal." The largest lump of gold found in California was found at Carson Hill. It weighed 195 pounds. Another, found at Magalia, weighed 54 pounds. The largest nugget on record is the "Welcome Stranger," which was found in 1869 in Victoria, Australia, only a few inches deep in a wagon rut. It weighed in at a hefty 208 pounds.

Is it true that the old time prospectors could tell what other metals were combined with gold in an ore sample simply from its color?

It is believed that gold was carried up from great depths, partly in solution, and later precipitated, at time in chemical combination with other minerals. In chemical combination, rather than in the "free state," gold can appear to be brown, black, purple, blue and even pink. Experienced prospectors were adept at "reading color." But it is also true that many of those hunting precious metals had no conception of their appearances as ore. The fellows who discovered the fabulous Comstock Lode shoveled tons of "bluish rock" into a gulch before learning that it assayed $1,600 per ton gold and $5,000 per ton silver!

Patterns, Trials, Major Errors

What is a pattern, and how does it differ from a pattern trial piece?

Doctor J. Hewitt Judd, a noted authority on pattern, experimental and trial pieces of U.S. coinage, defined patterns as: "Pieces which represent a new design, motto or denomination proposed for adoption as a regular issue, struck in the specified metal, and which were not adopted, at least in the same year." Pattern trial pieces differ from patterns in being struck in other than the specified metal.

What is an experimental piece, and how does it differ from an experimental trial piece?

Again quoting Dr. Judd: "Experimental pieces include those struck with any convenient dies to try out a new metal such as aluminum, a new alloy such as goloid, or a new denomination; those which represent a new shape such as the ring dollars; those which represent a new use of an accepted metal such as nickel for a ten-cent piece; and those representing changes in the planchets for the purpose of preventing counterfeiting, sweating, filing or clipping of the edges of the coins. When struck in the proper metal, where it is specified, these are experimental pieces; but struck in other metals, they are experimental trial pieces."

What is a die trial?

A die trial or die strike is an impression of an unfinished or completed die in a soft metal to test the die. The planchet utilized in the trial can be of any size or shape, and is usually struck on one side only, creating a uniface specimen.

Did the United States ever experiment with holed coins, and what was the intended purpose of them?

The United States struck patterns for perforated coins in 1849, '50, '52, '84 and '85. The center holes were of three types: round, square and denticulated. The denominations were 1 and 5 cents, and a gold dollar and half dollar.

Judging from the historical context of their time, it would appear that they were efforts to make a smaller coin of more precious metal (a holed billon cent to replace the large copper cent) or to increase the size of a coin of the same metallic content (a large holed silver nickel to replace the smaller silver half dime.)

The perforated gold patterns of the 1850s were a direct result of the California gold strike which caused the hoarding of silver coins by increasing the price of silver in relation to gold. Holed gold dollars and half dollars were proposed to alleviate the shortage of circulating coin; the holed center to increase the size of the coins to a more convenient dimension.

I have heard the term "double-struck coin." Would you please define it?

The double-struck coin results from a simple malfunctioning of the ejector system of a coin press, in consequence of which the coin is left in the collar to receive a second strike. If the position of the planchet is not disturbed, the second strike is imposed directly upon the first, and is not detectable. Should the planchet rotate between strikes, it receives two separate and distinct impressions. The value of a double-struck coin and off-center errors as well, is directly related to the degree of variation, with top value given to a 180 degree variation.

Clipped planchets and double strikes are not uncommon, but unusual in combination. Here, a piece of the planchet was clipped off when it was made. After being struck in the press, the coin did not eject properly and was partially struck again.

What is an off-center coin?

An off-center coin is created when a failure in the "layer-on" action of a coin press improperly seats a planchet so that only part of it receives the die impression. The value of this type error is directly related to the degree of off-centering. Minor off-centering (1 to 10 percent) occurs with routine frequency.

Are there such things as "off-metal" coins?

They are among the most coveted of Mint errors.

Off-metal or off-planchet coins are the inevitable consequence of the same coin press being used to strike several denominations of U.S. coins, as well as foreign coins. At the end of a minting run, an employee makes a cursory inspection of the hopper to see if any unstruck planchets remain. Occasionally one is overlooked. If the press is then switched to the minting of a different denomination, the result will be an off-metal coin, that is a cent struck on a dime planchet, etc. Harder to explain is the instance where a finished coin is restruck with the dies of a different denomination, such as the reported example of a Lincoln cent struck with the dies for a Liberty Standing quarter.

The government considers such errors to be unauthorized coinage, subject to confiscation.

Was the 1955 double date a double struck coin?

Not in the classical sense of being struck twice in different positions in the coin press. The error was caused by a misadventure in the making of the working or production die.

Several blows from a hub die are required during the die sinking process that produces a working die. The working die must be removed and annealed between strikes to prevent it from becoming work-hardened. If it is not replaced precisely in its previous position, the subsequent strike from the hub will be out of register, resulting in a working die with doubled impressions. About 20,000 1955 doubled-die cents were struck with such an improperly prepared die before the error was detected.

I have been told that the 1913 Liberty Head nickels are "pieces de caprice." What is meant by this?

A piece de caprice is an authorized piece struck for some reason other than as a pattern, experimental or trial piece — usually to satisfy a whim or create a rarity.

What is a "clover-leaf" error?

A major error of extreme rarity. It is a combination of major errors in being triple struck with a pair of off-center impressions, the resulting appearance being similar to that of a clover-leaf.

Can you tell me what is meant by a "Three-legged Buffalo"?

The term is used to describe a major error occurring on certain 1937-D nickels wherein the midsection of the buffalo's right foreleg is obliterated. It is believed that the error resulted when the die was ground down to remove injuries sustained when it accidentally clashed with the obverse die.

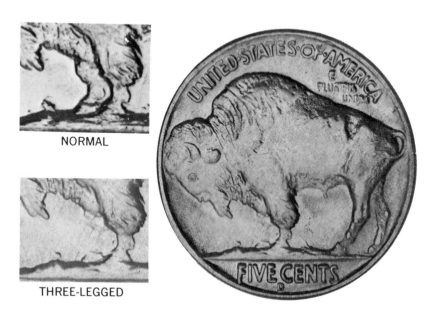

NORMAL

THREE-LEGGED

Other 1937-D nickels have been altered to simulate this prized error. There are many differences between the genuine error coin and the spurious ones. Among them, the hoof of the missing leg is visible, and the stump of the leg thins out before disappearing on the genuine coin. Altered specimens frequently show an abrupt, clean severance line, and no hoof. A line of tiny, rough dots extends from the belly of the buffalo to the ground on the genuine specimens.

What is considered to be the most improbable example of a multiple major-error coin?

A double-dated coin would certainly be one candidate for this honor.

In 1900, a properly struck 1899-dated Indian Head cent was channeled back into the coining process and fed into the coin press, resulting in an upside down, half off-center restrike bearing two different dates!

Minor Errors, Oddities and Varieties

I am confused by the seemingly endless variety of mint errors. Can you give me a breakdown of types?

Three major categories of errors are generally recognized: die errors, planchet errors, and striking errors. They are further subdivided as follows:

DIE ERRORS

1) Die breaks
2) Die cracks
3) Die gouges
4) Die scratches
5) Die clashes
6) Worn dies
7) Polished dies
8) Double and multiple mint marks
9) Engraving errors
10) Overdates
11) Shifting
12) Double entry of hub

PLANCHET ERRORS

1) Off metal
2) Wrong planchet
3) Poor alloy mix
4) Clipped planchets
5) Damaged planchets
6) Laminations
7) Split planchets
8) Blank planchets

STRIKING ERRORS

1) Doubling
2) Multiple strikes
3) Collar errors
4) Indented errors
5) Impressed errors
6) Off-center strikes
7) Edge strikes
8) Filled die
9) Misaligned die
10) Slipping-edge die
11) Die trial
12) Rotated die

As I was leaving my first coin club meeting, I heard a collector refer to another as a "fido" collector. What did he mean?

"FIDO" is a coined word frequently applied to mint errors. It is formed from the first letter of each of four words applicable to coins that deviate from a normal strike: Freaks, Imperfections, Defects and Oddities.

Can you account for the upsurge of interest in recent years in mint errors?

Major mint errors — overdates, off-center strikes, multiple-struck coins — have long been of great interest to most collectors. Some of the more significant minor errors — die breaks, double-dates, clips — have also enjoyed a small but enthusiastic following for many years.

The tremendous expansion of interest which occurred during the past few years, an interest which caused the formation of national error clubs, the appearance of regular error columns in the coin press, and a comprehensive cataloging of mint errors, is to a great extent due to the withdrawing and melting of the silver coins of the twentieth century.

Coin collecting attracts devotees from all levels of the social structure. Many collectors, particularly youngsters and those of modest financial means, were unable or unwilling to make substantial coin purchases. They derived their "kicks" from attempting to assemble their date-mint sets from circulating coins. The coin melt narrowed their activity to cents and nickels and the readily available clads. Many turned to errors, particularly in the Lincoln cent, as an inexpensive means to continued hobby enjoyment.

The increased availability of modern errors has also inadvertently exposed more collectors to the error field, and attracted their continuing interest. The tremendous increase in coin production in recent years has greatly increased the incidence of errors through overuse of dies, and the physical impossibility of detecting all errors by normal inspection procedures.

Are oddities and varieties in current coinage of the United States considered to be good collector items?

Any valid oddity or variety is considered to be a "good" collector item by one interested in the field. The true hobby collector, whatever his interest, does not confuse desirability with market value.

If by "good" you mean market value or investment potential, it can only be said that the current trend or catalog price of minor errors should be considered as guides, rather than firm value estimates. It would appear that a minor error or oddity is worth precisely what an interested party is willing to pay for it. As the interest in minor errors grows, a firm market will inevitably emerge as demand justifies it. At the present time, the majority of U.S. collectors are not minor-error buffs, and will not pay a premium for a coin on that basis alone.

Recently while checking an accumulation of cents, I found a number of examples on which various date numerals and legend letters appear to be filled, particularly the loop of the B, 9 and 6. What caused this, and is it a common occurrence?

This type of error is created when a small portion of the working die becomes fatigued and breaks away, leaving a hole into which the coin planchet metal is forced by the impact of striking, producing a raised, irregular feature on the coin surface. Die break errors of this type are very common today, and while they make interesting displays they are not generally valuable.

My father gave me a 1956-D Lincoln cent he received in change on which "Liberty" is misspelled LIBIERTY. Is this an engraver's error? Is it valuable?

Your cent is an example of the popular oddity known as the "BIE" error. It was caused when a portion of the die between B and E broke away, leaving a sharply delineated depression in the die which raised what appears to be an additional I in LIBERTY. The BIE error is quite common in its cruder expression; that is, with the extra I being generally featureless and of less than full height. They are of little value. However, examples where the I is attractively formed, such as the 1959-D BIE cent, have brought prices as high as $50.

I am familiar with the "Godless" coins of Canada, but what is an "atheist cent"?

The "atheist cent" is a major, and a valuable, example of a die break. A portion of the rim of a 1970-S cent die broke away, raising a "cud" on the coins that obliterated "We Trust" of the motto "In God We Trust." This error appears to have settled into the $50 class.

What is the cause of such unseemly oddities as the 1954 Roosevelt dime with the handlebar or Hitler mustache, and the 1955 Franklin "Bugs Bunny" half dollar?

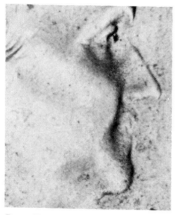

Bugs Bunny Half Mustache Dime

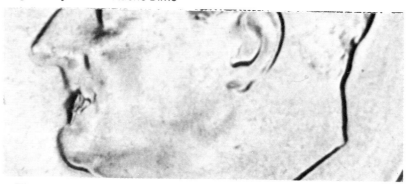

These curious oddities were created by unusual die deterioration which allowed the coin planchet metal to form unintended but humorous blobs on the surface of the coin; in the instance of the 1955 half dollar, giving Franklin a neat set of buckteeth. The 1954 dimes were notorious for this type of defect, producing in addition to the mustache varieties, fangs, warts, cowlicks, broken nose, and occasional combinations of these oddities.

At a coin show I saw a small exhibit labeled "The Wandering Ds of '56." It consisted of a large number of 1956-D cents on which the D mint mark was erratically positioned. Some were left, right, up, down, even tilted and doubled. Can you explain the erratic positioning of the mint mark?

The only design feature of the working die which historically was not impressed by hubbing is the mint mark. Until recent years mint marks were always hand-punched into each die manufactured at the Philadelphia Mint, just prior to when they were shipped to the branch mints. Human error account for the lack of total uniformity in its positioning.

Double or multiple mint marks resulted from the punch being applied more than once with improper alignment with the initial punch impression. Doubled vertical mint marks are of little value unless the doubling is bold. Rare examples which combine a vertical and horizontal mint mark, or consist of the mark of one mint being struck over the mark of another, are status errors that command substantial premiums.

I have a number of 1943 steel coins on which the "4" of 1943 is either weak or missing. What caused this?

The missing or weak numeral (or letter) error is generally caused by the concerned recessed area of the die filling with dirt, grease or metal particles, preventing coin planchet metal from flowing into that area and raising the intended numeral or letter.

Weak and small numerals and letters, and missing minor design details, can also be caused by a portion of the die being removed or weakened when the die was polished, or by a die excessivly worn by overuse.

I have seen coins that appear to have a bite taken out of them. How did this occur, and what is their value?

These "bitten" coins are called "clips." They occur during the blanking operation where a group of circular cutters punches planchets from a strip of metal. If the strip of metal fails to advance properly, each punch will overlap the last, and the consequent blanks will appear to have a bite taken out of them. If the strip is moved too far to either side, or if the punching proceeds to the end of the strip, a flat or edge clip will result.

While the value of clips, and other minor errors, is mainly determined by how badly someone wants it, large clips, multiple clips, and clipped coins of the older types and higher denominations command greater premiums. All else being equal, the clipped coin that retains its date is of greater value.

How can I tell a mint-made clip from one made in someone's garage?

The homemade clip, produced by punching out a bit of the metal with a round punch die, will show a flattened or buckled effect on the side of the coin opposite to that upon which the punch was applied. The rim of a genuine clip will taper off as it approaches the clipped area due to the free flow of metal in that direction during the striking process.

I have a nickel which has what appears to be a short length of wire firmly imbedded in Jefferson's cheek. Could this have happened at the Mint?

Error collectors will assure you that anything can happen at the mint. Your nickel is representative of the type of error known as an impressed error, and reflects the fact that a scrap of wire was between the coin planchet and obverse die at the time the coin was struck.

I have a naturally dark (not tarnished) Jefferson nickel. What caused the discoloration? Is it valuable?

Off-color Jefferson nickels are not uncommon, and are known in hues ranging from smoky blue through deep purple to black. The discoloration is caused by an incorrect alloy mix containing significantly too much copper. Some collectors are attracted to them, as some prefer toned proof coins, and will pay a small premium for them.

The discoloration of poor alloy mix is more commonly encountered in the bronze cent, taking the form of coins with discernible yellow streaks or with a distinct yellowish cast. The coin is normally composed of 95 per cent copper and 5 per cent zinc. As the proportion of zinc to copper increases, the coins become progressively more yellow, until at a ratio of 30 to 70 per cent the alloy becomes ordinary brass.

All of the United States coins I have ever seen have the reverse rotated 180 degrees in relation to the obverse. However, today I found a Lincoln cent which has the reverse rotated 90 degrees. How did this come about, and what is such a coin worth?

When the dies are attached to a coining press, they are locked in proper alignment with a key. Sometimes a key will be improperly locked or will work loose, allowing a die to rotate away from its proper position and permit the striking of rotated die errors. The value of such oddities is determined by the degree of rotation involved, and by the type and denomination of the affected coin. The premium paid for coins of modest variance and low denomination is relatively low.

What is meant by a "first process" blank planchet coin and a "second process"?

First process blanks are characterized by their sharp edges. Second process blanks have had their edges upset so that they are slightly higher than the surface of the blank and slightly smaller in diameter than the finished coin would be. Unmilled and milled would be more precise classifications.

What is a die trial as it relates to error coinage?

The "die trial" error is a very weak strike caused by the dies being set too far apart during the adjustment process, or by the planchet being struck by a press slowing to a stop. The design features appear weak. This error should not be confused with the die trial piece produced by the impression of an unfinished or completed die in soft metal to test the die.

Confederate Coins And Paper Money

What is the difference between "Confederate Money" and "Southern States Currency"?

"Confederate Money" is considered to be that issued by the Confederate States of America or any of the constituent states during the period of the Civil War. "Southern States Currency" in its broadest definition includes any money issued by any of the Southern states before, during and after the Civil War.

Is the Confederate half dollar a genuine coin?

The Confederacy planned to issue a coinage using the facilities of the New Orleans Mint. Only one die was ever prepared, a half-dollar reverse depicting the Confederate Seal. This was muled with an obverse die for the U.S. 1861-O half dollar to produce four pattern strikes, which comprise the extent of Confederate coinage.

In 1879, J. W. Scott purchased the original reverse die and obtained five hundred 1861-O half dollars. He shaved the reverse from each of the coins, and in its place impressed the Confederate Seal with the original die. These "restrikes" are the Confederate half dollars in collections today. Scott also struck five hundred specimens in white metal, using the Confederate die to fashion the obverse and his own store card for the reverse.

Incidentally, in 1861 the seceded state of Louisiana the Confederacy also caused to be struck 2,202,633 half dollars which are "genuine" to the extent that they owe their origin to the auspices of the Confederacy. However, they were struck with the confiscated equipment and dies of the U.S. branch mint at New Orleans, and cannot be distinguished from the 1861-O half dollars struck by the U.S. before the seizure.

Did the Confederate States ever issue their own one-cent pieces?

No, but they tried. In 1861, Bailey & Co., Philadelphia jewelers, agreed to supply a minor coinage for the Confederacy and engaged the well-known engraver Robert Lovett Jr. to prepare the dies. Lovett executed dies for a cent piece, employing on obverse the same turbaned Liberty Head he had created for a Northern store card, and on reverse a wreath of cotton, sugar cane and tobacco enclosing the words 1 CENT. He placed the small initial L on a bale of cotton at the bottom of the wreath. After striking a dozen specimens in copper-nickel, he had second thoughts about giving aid to the enemy, and hid the dies and coins.

They were eventually purchased by John Haseltine who, in 1874 caused the striking of 7 cents in gold, 12 in silver, and 55 in copper before the dies broke. In 1962, Robert Bashlow, using a transfer die, struck 30,000 specimens in platinum, silver, goldine and bronze, which can be easily distinguished from the "original" restrikes by the presence of heavy die cracks on both the obverse and reverse. He then presented the original and transfer dies to the Smithsonian Institution.

I have seen advertised Confederate dimes, half dimes, etc., yet they are not listed in coin catalogs. Why?

These are "fantasy" pieces of post-Civil War vintage created by an imaginative coin dealer. They have no authentic connection with the Confederacy, and are not genuine coins. They exist in a variety of metals and denominations, and generally state the denomination fractionally, as 1/10, etc.

I have a Confederate $5 note. Is it rare?

Probably not. All genuine Confederate notes have a collector value but in the majority of instances it is a nominal one. Strangely, Confederate currency has not enjoyed the prestige arbitrarily bestowed upon Colonial or Continental Currency, and broken bank notes.

The most highly prized types of Confederate currency are the 1861 Montgomery notes issued at the first Confederate capital, although there are rarer individual notes of subsequent issues.

The notes commonly encountered were issued at Richmond, the permanent capital. They are distinguished by their pink obverse and blue reverse. The last Richmond issue of 1864 was printed in astronomical quantities necessitated by the extreme depreciation of the purchasing power of the Confederate dollar. These notes were secured by a pledge to redeem in Confederate stocks and bonds two years after ratification of a treaty of peace between the Confederacy and the United States. In short, they were secured by a fading hope, for by late 1864 the most dedicated adherents to the Southern cause regarded the prospect of Southern victory to be as remote as the arrival of a voyager from Andromeda.

Large quantities of the 1864 issue survived the war to be distributed across the country as curios and premiums, which largely accounts for their prevalence today.

Why didn't the Confederate States of America issue coins?

On March 9, 1861, the Confederate Congress enacted legislation providing for continued operation of the New Orleans Mint, seized by southern forces on Jan. 31, 1861, and the Charlotte and Dahlonega Mints seized subsequently instructing that dies be prepared "for the coin of the Confederate States." However, it was quickly determined that the South did not have sufficient bullion to implement the Act in a meaningful manner. Thereupon it was decided to reserve existing bullion to the Government for its necessities, and by Act of May 14, Congress declared "That from & after June 1st operations of the several mints in the Confederate States shall be suspended.

Is it true that Northern note companies engraved plates for Confederate and Southern States currency during the Civil War?

Notes are known bearing the name of the American Bank Note Co. and the National Bank Note Co., both of New York. The American Bank Note Co. had a branch at New Orleans. It is possible that it printed notes at New Orleans during the early part of the war under the name of the Southern Bank Note Co. (a name that appears on many note issues, although the company was not listed in the New Orleans directory) to conceal the fact that the notes were engraved by Northern engravers of a firm with a branch doing business in the South.

Is it true that Confederate paper money was not printed on watermarked paper?

No. Confederate notes were printed on both marked and unmarked paper. The most frequently encountered watermark consists of the initials "C.S.A." (Confederate States of America) in block or script letters. The watermarks "FIVE" and "TEN" frequently appear on notes of like denominations. Among the rarely found watermarks are "N.Y." in block letters extending nearly the width of the note, and "Hodgkinson & Co. Wookey Hole Mills," the mark of an English paper mill. Watermarks can also be found on notes issued by the individual states of the Confederacy.

What can you tell me about the popular Confederate note known as the "Sweet Potato" note?

Your reference is to the $10 Richmond note dated Sept. 2, 1861, the central design of which is known as "General Marion's Sweet Potato Dinner." The design of this note, engraved by B. Duncan, Columbia, South Carolina, was taken from a famous painting by John R. White of Charleston, South Carolina, which depicts an authentic incident in the military career of Francis

Marion the "Swamp Fox," who was one of the originators of guerrilla warfare and a hero of the Southern campaigns of the American Revolution. After futilely trying to trap Marion's guerrilla army in the swamps of South Carolina, British Colonel Banistree "Bloody" Tarleton asked him for a truce. Marion responded by inviting his enemy to dinner at his swamp camp. Instead of the lavish display of Southern hospitality he expected, Tarleton found only a dinner of sweet potatoes served on a bare table in a swamp. He later reported to General Cornwallis that if the colonists were willing to fight without pay, proper clothes or food, "they could not be conquered."

This design is not unique to Confederate currency. It was previously used by the Bank of the State of South Carolina on $5 notes issued in 1853 and 1861.

I have heard that the shortage of skilled note engravers in the South was so critical that engravers had to be "imported," or the plates engraved in the North and abroad. Wasn't the lack of engravers in the South insurance against counterfeiting of the notes?

Because of the lack of skilled craftsmen, equipment and materials, few, if any, illicit notes were made in the South. Confederate currency was, however, extensively counterfeited in Louisville, New York City, Philadelphia, and Havanna, Cuba. Efforts to prevent counterfeiting by the use of watermarked bank note paper, or by using pink paper or printing the notes in multiple colors were ineffective. By the last year of the war, the supply of currency, swollen by counterfeits, was so over-abundant in the South that steps had to be taken to retire part of it from circulation.

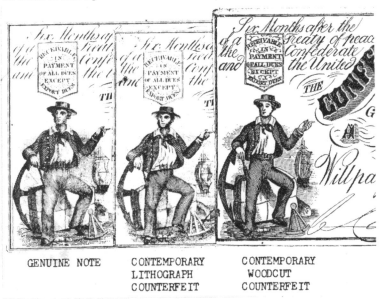

GENUINE NOTE   CONTEMPORARY   CONTEMPORARY
                 LITHOGRAPH   WOODCUT
                 COUNTERFEIT   COUNTERFEIT

I have heard the name of Samuel C. Upham of Philadelpia mentioned in discussions of Confederate paper money. What did a presumably loyal Northerner have to do with Confederate currency?

Although Upham, a Philadelphia stationer, never represented himself as a counterfeiter, he was the most famous of the many printers of spurious Confederate currency notes. He called his excellent replicas "fac-similes" and "mementos of the rebellion," and furnished them to the trade, ostensibly as curiosities, at a cost of 50 cents per 100 notes, regardless of denomination. The dealers in turn sold them to interested parties for one cent each. Upham printed 28 different facsimiles of Rebel notes and shinplasters, and 15 different postage stamps during this period of March 12, 1862 to August 1, 1863. By his account, he produced a total of 1,564,050 facsimile Confederate notes in denominations of from 5 cents to 100 dollars.

Although Upham's notes were clearly marked on margin "Fac-simile Confederate notes sold wholesale or retail, by S. C. Upham, 403 Chestnut Street, Phila., Pa.," they, in the words of Confederate Senator Foote, "injured the Confederate cause more than General McClellan and his army." Large quantities of his notes with the "fac-simile" notice clipped off were smuggled into the South and placed in circulation, generally through the purchase of cotton from Rebel planters.

How much money did the Confederacy issue during the Civil War?

The exact amount can not be determined. Little effort was made to keep an accurate record of the amount issued after July, 1864. The amount authorized by the various acts approximates $1.5 billion. To this must be added the amount of the issues of the individual states, as well as the amount issued by railroads, insurance companies, merchants, counties and towns. The grand total was probably close to $2.5 billion.

Can money issued by the Confederate States of America be redeemed for current money?

Redemption is specifically forbidden by Section 4 of the 14th Amendment to the Constitution which states: "Neither the United States nor any State shall assume or pay any debt or obligation incurred in aid of insurrection or rebellion against the United States, or any claim for the loss or emancipation of any slave; but all such debts, obligations and claims shall be held illegal and void."

United States Paper Money

I have a $5 bill issued on a home town bank. It not only has the signatures of the "Register of the Treasury" and the "Treasurer of the United States", but is signed by local bank officials, the "Cashier" and "President," as well. Is it any good?

Take all you can get. You have a National Bank Note that is as sound as the day it was printed.

In 1862, as part of a program to revise and stabilize chaotic banking standards, the Federal Government began granting charters to banks able to deposit "blue chip" government bonds as security. Concurrently, the right of State Banks to issue currency was revoked.

From 1862 to 1933, when the privilege of National Banks to issue currency was terminated, 14,348 National Banks were authorized to issue National Bank Notes with exquisitely drafted, historically attuned designs, many of which, due to rarity and artistic appeal, command a collector premium substantially in excess of their face value.

I have several Silver Certificates and Federal Reserve Notes and one or two notes with red seals, including some $2 U.S. Notes that have red seals. All are of the same size and similar in design to the notes we get from banks today. The other day I found a brown seal note that had the name of a bank from a neighboring town on it. Is it any good?

It is, as are all paper notes issued by the U.S. since 1861. You have a National Bank Note. Notes bearing brown seals were issued prior to 1933 under provisions of the National Bank Act. There are also small-size gold certificates, making a total of five different types of notes.

What can you tell me about a funny little 50¢ bill I have?

Your "funny little 50¢ bill" is a piece of the Fractional Currency that replaced the Postage Currency in 1862. It can still be redeemed for face value, although if you did so someone else would do the laughing, for it is worth a substantial premium to collectors.

Fractional Currency notes were issued in a variety of designs in denominations of 3¢, 5¢, 10¢, 25¢ and 50¢ from 1862 to 1878.

I have a 5¢ Fractional Currency note that looks like it has a picture of one of the Smith Brothers on it. I don't recognize him. Who is he?

His name is Spencer Clark, and he is remembered by collectors as the man responsible for our coins and paper notes not bearing portraits of the living.

It is believed that the 5¢ note of the type you possess (issued in June, 1864) was intended to bear the portrait of the soldier-explorer George Rogers Clark. But Spencer Clark, a civil servant in the Treasury Department, who at the time held the post of superintendent of the "National Currency Bureau," the first person to hold that post, had his likeness put on the note instead. This presumptuous act angered Congress, and resulted in the passage of a law prohibiting the likeness of a living person from appearing on U.S. money thereafter.

What is a "jackass note"?

The note referred to is the Legal Tender Note of 1869 and subsequent series of 1875, 1878 and 1880. All have an eagle on the obverse which, when the note is inverted for viewing upside down, resembles the head of a "jackass."

What is the highest denomination note circulated by the U.S. government?

Generally speaking, the $1,000 value is the highest face value that might be encountered in circulation. Actually, no notes with face values higher than $100 have been printed since 1945, and since 1969 all higher value notes have been subject to permanent retirement as they circulate back into the Federal Reserve System.

While a quantity (42,000) $100,000 notes were printed in the 1934 Gold Certificate series, these were prepared for exclusive use within the nation's banking system at the federal level. Otherwise, the highest denominations printed and released for circulation were $5,000 and $10,000 notes.

In the large size currency era the $5,000 and $10,000 values were issued as series 1878 Legal Tender Notes, series 1918 Federal Reserve Notes and series 1882 and 1888 Gold Certificates. The 5,000 unit was also issued as a three year interest bearing note under a July 17, 1861, Congressional authorization, while a 1900 dated $10,000 Gold Certificate series was also printed.

In the small size currency era $5,000 notes exist dated 1928 in the Federal Reserve Note and Gold Certificate series, and dated 1934 in the Federal Reserve Note series only. The $10,000 value was issued in both series bearing both dates.

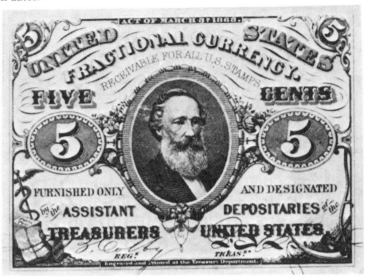

Five cents fractional currency note featuring the portrait of Spencer Clark still is worth a nickel in redemption, but no collector would be foolish enough to sell it for such a pittance. Earlier postage currency (below) was issued in sheets, perforated like stamps, for easy tearing.

I have a $5 bill that has the word "Hawaii" printed on both the front and back. Can you tell me what I have, and its value?

You have one of the special Hawaiian precautionary notes introduced in the islands after the Japanese attack on Pearl Harbor. The Hawaiian series was printed in $1 Silver Certificates and $5, $10 and $20 San Francisco Federal Reserve Notes. The notes carried brown Treasury Seals, rather than blue or green, and were overprinted with HAWAII in small letters on both sides of the obverse, and in large, openface capital letters on the reverse. The purpose of the overprint was to distinguish the paper money in use on Hawaii, and by troops stationed elsewhere in the Pacific theater, to facilitate its invalidation should it fall into enemy hands.

The series 1934 $5 and $20 are considered quite scarce. The 1935 A $1 and 1934 A $5, $10 and $20 all demand a premium. These bills are still legal tender.

Hawaii overprints with brown seals were issued just after Pearl Harbor for use in the islands. If the Japanese had invaded Hawaii, the distinctive notes could have been devalued with a minimum of confusion.

I have two dollar bills signed by Granahan and Dillon which look alike. The only difference is one is series 1935-H and the other 1957-B. Why are these two series designations used?

The difference between 1935 and 1957 series notes is negligible but positive. Series 1935 notes are printed on paper that is millwet and contains 50 percent cotton and 50 percent linen. The subsequent drying process imparts a slight wrinkling to the notes. Series 1957 notes are dry-printed using paper that is 75 percent cotton and 25 percent linen. This process produces flat, wrinkle-free notes.

A friend of mine who runs a retail shop dutifully checks the receipts at the end of each day looking for "rare Barr notes." How rare are they? What are they worth?

Joseph W. Barr served as secretary of the Treasury for only a month, from December 20, 1968, to January 20, 1969. Despite this short tenure, more than 470 million of the Barr-Granahan dollar bills were printed, or more than two for every man, woman and child in the United States. Uncirculated Barr notes have a minimal value.

Why are the signatures of Granahan and Dillon on notes dated 1935?

Unlike coins, paper money is not dated for the year of its issue. The year 1935 refers to the date the basic design of the note was first used. The alphabetic suffix, in this case H, denotes a minor change, usually a new Secretary of Treasury, or Treasurer of the U.S., or both.

What do all those little numbers in the series 1957 one-dollar bills mean; i.e., A1, C3, D4, B2, etc.?

This particular note is printed in a 32 subject sheet. Each quarter has a numerical designation: 1, 2, 3, 4. Each numerical designation has an alphabetic designation to locate a particular note in relation to all others. The designations reveal the exact location on the 32 subject sheet from which the individual note came.

I have always understood that whenever there was any change in the design of a U.S. currency note the suffix letter of the series designation was changed. However, I have two series 1935 G $1 Silver Certificates which differ from each other. One has the motto, "In God We Trust," while the other does not. Can you explain why the suffix letter is the same on both notes?

No, but we are not alone. Normally the second variety of the series 1935 G note would have carried a new designation (H), but for some unexplained reason the change was not made. The second variety is generally considered to be the scarcer of the two.

I am confused about the appearance of the national motto, "In God We Trust," on our paper currency. Can you tell me the why and the where of it?

The Act requiring that the national motto appear on U.S. paper currency was signed by the President on July 11, 1955. It first appeared on $1 Silver Certificates dated 1957. It was not initially intended that the motto be added to the series 1935 Silver Certificates, but they, too, were converted in 1962, without the traditional change of suffix letter.

It was not until March of 1964 that the motto was added to other denominations, in this case the fives and twos. It was added at that time in accordance with a conversion schedule announced early in 1964 which called for a complete conversion through the one hundred dollar denomination by January of 1965.

Popular with paper money collectors are the three silver certificates known as the "educational" series. On the $1 note, History instructs youth, with the Constitution at right, the Capitol and Washington Monument in the background; Science presents the twin gifts of steam and electricity to Commerce and Manufacture on the $2 note, and the $5 denomination depicts Electricity as the dominant force in the world.

Is it illegal to hold Gold Certificates?

Gold Certificates were called in the same as gold coin by the order of the Secretary of the Treasury, dated December 28, 1933; at that time, it was illegal to hold them, However, the Secret Service did not come looking for them because they could not be exchanged for gold and were not legal tender, although they were exchangeable for lawful money at any bank.

In April, 1964, the Treasury Department revised its ruling, and it is now legal to own and display Gold Certificates for numismatic purposes.

I recently took some Silver Certificates to the Treasury in Washington thinking to redeem them for silver dollars, as the obligation of the notes pledged. I was informed that the Treasury is no longer obligated to redeem the notes with either silver dollars or silver bullion. Why can't the government be held to its obligation?

Prior to 1935 the government was obligated to redeem Silver Certificates with silver dollars, and thereafter with one dollar in silver bullion, which at the pegged silver price of $1.2929 per ounce amounted to .77 ounce of silver bullion per dollar. The traditional tie between silver and our circulating currency came to an end on June 24, 1968. Congress, by the Act of June 24, 1967, provided one year for the redemption of Silver Certificates. During that period notes to the amount of $150 million were redeemed, leaving approximately $245 million of Silver Certificates which the government is no longer obligated to redeem, although they remain valid legal tender. The retired Silver Certificates have been replaced by Federal Reserve Notes.

I have a $20 bill that was partly destroyed by burning. Can I exchange it for a new one?

Three fifths or more of a mutilated bill will be redeemed by the Treasurer of the United States at full face value. Less than three fifths, but more than two fifths, will be redeemed at one-half face value. Fragments not more than two-fifths will not be redeemed unless accompanied by proof, in the form of affidavits, that the missing portions have been destroyed. Your bank will redeem the note.

Is it legal to photograph coins or paper money?

Coins can be reproduced on flat surfaces; that is, they must not have a relief.

Laws pertaining to illustrations of paper money were liberalized on Sept. 2, 1958. "Printed illustrations of paper money, checks, bonds and other obligations and securities of the United States and foreign governments are permissible for numismatic, educational, historical and newsworthy purposes. The illustrations of paper money, checks or bonds must be in black and white, and must be of a size less than three fourths or more than one and one half times the size of the genuine. No illustrations may be in color."

These restrictions have been challenged in recent years. As recently as 1984, the U.S. Supreme Court has upheld their validity insofar as the size restrictions and use of color are concerned.

What is the rarest $2 note issued?

There are two possible answers to this question. Authorities generally concede that the series 1878 Legal Tender deuce signed by Glenni W. Scofield as Register of the Treasury and James Gilfillan as Treasurer of the U.S. is the rarest in terms of availability. The original issue National Bank Note series, however, features the popular "Lazy 2" note, which in the Noah L. Jeffries, F. E. Spinner signature combination generally commands the higher premium when sold.

How many notes are there in a complete type set of $2 bills?

Introduction of the new series 1976 Federal Reserve Note deuce brought to 17 the number of basic type notes in this denomination which have been issued under the authority of the federal government since the first modern circulating paper money issues were authorized in 1861. Of this total, 13 were issued during the period of large size note issues (1861-1923); five in the Legal Tender or U.S. Note sizes, four Silver Certificates, two Treasury of Coin Notes, and one each in the National Bank Note and Federal Reserve Bank Note series. Three small size United States Note issues preceded the new 1976 bicentennial oriented issue.

Undoubtedly the most popular type note, and the best known aside from the distinctive "Lazy 2" is the series 1896 Silver Certificate, one of three notes in the "educational" series. This note portrays science presenting steam and electricity to commerce and industry on the face side, while the reverse presents vignette portraits of inventors Robert Fulton and Samuel Morse.

Why are U.S. $2 notes no longer being actively printed and circulated? It seems that, with the $1 bill steadily declining in purchasing power, a $2 note would be a practical alternative.

The U.S. Treasury came to the same conclusion a few years, and a new $2 note was scheduled to enter commercial channels on April 13, 1976. Except for series (1976), signatures, and designation as a Federal Reserve note, the face of the new paper $2 was similar to its predecessor. However, the back presented a view of John Trumbull's painting, the Signing of the Declaration of Independence, rather than the picture of Jefferson's home, Monticello.

Reproduction of Trumbull's painting shows delegates to the Continental Congress and Thomas Jefferson presenting the Declaration of Independence for signatures. In adapting the scene to the back of the $2 note, the Treasury cropped six delegates from the original, an omission that triggered protests from some historians.

The old $2 note, last printed in 1965, was discontinued for a variety of reasons, both practical and frivolous. Merchants and consumers complained because the denomination could be confused with the $1, and tradesmen objected because standard cash registers contained no provisions for the odd value. Superstition and myth also entered the picture; some despised the two-spot because of its reputation as a convenient monetary instrument at race tracks and in brothels. Conversely, some habitues of the tracks wouldn't place a bet with the deuce because it was "bad luck."

Probably the biggest disadvantage was the small volume printed. In 1965, only 3.2 million were produced, and only 21 million were printed in the preceding two years.

No such problem can be attributed to the failure of the 1976 issue, as the Treasury produced about 400 million pieces by June 30, 1976. Subsequent printings, by reducing need for the $1 denomination, would have saved more than $5 million annually in costs to the government, officials estimated. However, the issue was almost totally shunned by the public.

A friend of mine has a one-dollar note with a beautiful blue reverse. How come?

The green pigment in the ink used to print the backs of U.S. paper money has blue and yellow components. If a printed note is exposed to acid or even acid fumes, the yellow component may be destroyed, thus turning the color of the ink to blue. If the green-colored note is exposed to an alkali, the blue component may be destroyed, turning the color of the ink to yellow. These color changes can be brought about either accidentally or intentionally, but there is no known case of the color change having taken place within the Bureau of Engraving and Printing.

Peroxide will turn a note yellow within a very few minutes. A note left in clothing being laundered can be turned yellow by the alkali present in the washing product. A note carried in the pocket of anyone working with acid, or in an environment of acid fumes, can be turned blue. Needless to say, the change of color can also be obtained by deliberately exposing a note to acid or alkali. Your friend's "blue-back" note has no premium value because the change was achieved after the note was placed in circulation, and it is therefore not a printing error.

I have read of "mule" coins that bear a mismatched obverse and reverse. Does this type of error occur in paper money?

Yes, but infrequently. Notes with $5 face and $10 back, $10 face and $5 back, and $10 face and $1 back are known. They are valued between several hundred and a few thousand dollars in new condition.

Error notes identified as offset printings, double printings, ink smears, incomplete printings, printings on foreign matter, board breaks, folded sheets, off-register printings, torn-paper printings, inverted printings, missing overprints, incomplete overprints, double overprints, overprints on incorrect side, cutting errors and mismatched serial numbers are also known. Many carry substantial premiums. Apparent errors can also be manufactured through the careful application of a good eraser.

Is it true that the U.S. issued a special Federal Reserve $1 note to mark the assassination of President Kennedy in Dallas, Texas, on November 22, 1963?

The facts of the so-called "assassination note" are as follows: The note does bear the date 1963 (year of Kennedy's assassination). It does carry the figure "11" four times (month of the assassination). It does carry the identification "Dallas, Texas" (city of assassination). It does carry a large letter "K" within a circle on obverse, (eleventh letter in the alphabet), and in front of each serial number. None of these markings have any connection whatsoever with Kennedy's death.

The date "1963" is simply the series date. The letter "K" does not stand for "Kennedy," but does identify the Dallas Federal Reserve Bank as being in the 11th Federal Reserve District. The figure "11" also represents the Federal Reserve District of this instance. "Dallas, Texas" appears on all Federal Reserve notes issued by the Dallas Federal Reserve Bank.

This 1815 dated U.S. Treasury note, bearing the denominational value $10, was an interest bearing (7-percent) issue.

Why did the United States wait until 1861 before issuing paper money?

It didn't. It is true that paper money as we know it began with the "green-backs" of 1861, but the government did issue interest-bearing Treasury Notes during times of excessive Treasury drain, such as the War of 1812, the Mexican War of 1846, the depression years of 1837-43, the Panic of 1857, and during the unsettled years immediately prior to the Civil War. With the exception of the low denomination notes of 1815, which were not interest-bearing and circulated briefly, these Treasury Notes generally did not circulate as money and were quickly retired.

The "greenbacks" of 1861 were necessitated to meet Union military expenses of $3.5 million a day, at a time when tax revenues amount to but a third of that requirement.

I have a Federal Reserve Note that has a star * in place of the last letter of the serial number. What does it denote?

The star * indicated that the original note was destroyed in the printing process or was deleted by inspection and was replaced by a star * series note. The symbol is also utilized when the numbering machines reach 100,000,000 as the machines carry only eight digits. Instead of the usual prefix letter, the star * appears with the serial number on Gold Certificates, United States Notes and Silver Certificates; it appears in place of the suffix letter when used on Federal Reserve Notes and Federal Reserve Bank Notes. No star * notes were used in conjunction with National Bank Notes. The star * on the face of Treasury Notes is a decorative embellishment, and does not denote a replacement note.

Is it true that the song "Dixie" had its origin in a 10-dollar bill?

Dixie as a collective noun indicating the Southern states is thought to have originated from the practice of the Citizens Bank of Louisiana of printing "Dix" (10 in French) on 10-dollar bills as a convenience to that state's large French-speaking population. Thus, the south was the land of "Dixies."

My father left me a $1,000 bill issued by the Bank of the United States. It is printed on authentic parchment and bears the serial number 8894. A dealer told me it's a fake. Is he right?

Replica would be a better word. Several years ago a chemist discovered a chemical solution that gives vegetables membrane paper the appearance of old parchment. He formed a company to manufacture replicas of famous U.S. documents, and also produced replicas of paper money used during the Colonial, Revolutionary and Civil War periods. The most notorious of his numismatic replicas is a $1,000 note of the Bank of the United States numbered 8894.

I have a note classified as obsolete that has a pattern of rather large holes punched in it. Does this lessen the value of the note?

The punch holes are almost certainly cancellation marks indicating that the note was redeemed for face value by the issuer. Such notes generally bring less than unmarked specimens.

What is the origin of the dollar sign ($) and why doesn't it appear on United States paper money?

Three theories have been advanced to explain the origin of the dollar sign: 1) It was derived from the ribbon entwined Pillars of Hercules on the Spanish dollar, 2) It is a monogram combination of the letters "U" and "S" of United States, 3) It is a modification of the old Mexican symbol "Ps" for pesos. The third theory is generally assumed to be correct.

The dollar sign is not an official requirement of United States currency, the practice being to indicate the value in word form. The sign frequently appears on federal postage, revenue and fee stamps, and can be found on the $1000, $5000 and $10,000 denomination notes of Series 1918 Federal Reserve notes, but it has never appeared on any piece of paper money of the denominations issued for general circulation.

What is the significance of the large "eye" in a triangle appearing above an unfinished pyramid on the back of the dollar bill?

The complete device to which you refer is the reverse of the Great Seal of the United States. The eye in a triangle surrounded by a glory proper represents the Eye of Providence.

I understand that the small-size Legal Tender one-dollar note has a red seal, but I have never seen a dollar bill with a red seal in circulation. What happened to them?

The one-dollar Legal Tender note of Series 1928 is the only small-size note of that denomination to bear a red seal. The notes were released mainly in Puerto Rico years after they were printed, and are no longer in circulation.

Many collectors of small-size currency notes of the United States try to obtain a specimen of each of the Treasurer of the United States-Secretary of the Treasury signature combinations. Has the signature of these two officials always appeared on small-size notes?

A distinctive feature of the Series 1929 National Currency notes is the use of a Register of the Treasury-Treasurer of the United States signature combination.

National Currency notes and Federal Reserve Bank notes both carry the designation NATIONAL CURRENCY at top of the face of the note. Is there any way to quickly distinguish between the two types of notes?

Federal Reserve Bank notes are easily distinguished from National Currency notes by the presence in four positions on the face of the notes of the bank's district letter, and by the addition of OR BY LIKE DEPOSIT OF OTHER SECURITIES to the bonding statement at top of the face, in addition to the name of the bank being spelled out.

Small-size Federal Reserve notes were first issued in 1929. Why is it that the one-dollar bill so essential to everyday commerce wasn't issued until 1963?

One-dollar Federal Reserve notes weren't required until the issuing of one-dollar Silver Certificates was discontinued in 1963.

I know how to tell a Federal Reserve note from a Federal Reserve Bank note, but there must be a fundamental difference related to the economic system. What is it?

Federal Reserve notes are issues of the Federal Reserve System. Federal Reserve Bank notes are the issues of the individual banks within the system.

I have heard paper money collectors speak of "Experimental Issue notes." What are they?

In 1944, the Treasury Department released an experimental issue of Series 1935-A ONE DOLLAR Silver Certificates bearing an overprint of "R" (regular) or "S" (special) at lower right of the Treasury Seal. The purpose of the issue was to test the wearing qualities of regular and a special experimental currency paper. Results of the test were inconclusive, and the regular paper was continued in use.

Why do some of the $1, $5 and $10 small-size Silver Certificates have yellow Seals and blue serial numbers instead of the usual blue Seals and numbers?

A special issue of Silver Certificates was printed in 1942 for use during the North African campaign of World War II. These notes retained the customary blue serial numbers of Silver Certificates, but the Treasury Seal was printed a distinctive yellow to permit ready identification and demonetization of the notes in the event of military reverses. These specially marked notes were also used briefly during the 1943 assault on Sicily.

I know that Continental Currency and Broken Bank notes were issued in a variety of odd denominations, but is it true that the United States once issued a $3 Legal Tender note?

It is true that a Legal Tender specimen note of $3 denomination does exist, but notes of that denomination were never issued for circulation. Legal Tender notes of the Second Issue, dated August 1, 1862, were issued in denominations of $1 and $2 only. But interestingly, the face design of these notes includes the numerals 1, 2 and 3 in a vertical linear arrangement with the denomination numeral of the note encircled. Inclusion of the numeral 3 in this device indicates that a $3 note was also contemplated.

What is the "Technicolor Note" of 1905?

The Series 1905 $20 Gold Certificate has the center of the face gold tinted and the Seals and serial numbers printed in red, resulting in a spectacular color combination of gold, red, black and white.

I have been told that there is a United States bank note on which coin illustrations are used to indicate the value and series date. Do you know which note this is?

The back design of the $5 note of the Second Issue large-size Silver Certificate of the series of 1886 features five actual-size facsimile Morgan silver dollars. The coin at the center is dated 1886. There is another popular example of coins on bank notes. All of the National Gold Bank notes have on the back an illustration of an assortment of gold coins having a total face value of $211.

Has the United States ever issued a commemorative currency note?

None has ever been officially designated as such although the Series 1976 Federal Reserve note with a portrait of Thomas Jefferson on the face and a reproduction of Trumbull's painting of the signing of the Declaration of Independence on the back that was issued on Jefferson's birthday, during the nation's Bicentennial celebration, would be difficult to classify in any other manner. By the timing of their issuance, collectors also consider three large-size Silver Certificates — the $2 note of Series 1886 bearing the portrait of General Winfield Scott Hancock, the $2 note of Series 1891 bearing the portrait of secretary of the Treasury William Windom, and the $10 note of Series 1886 and 1908 bearing the portrait of Vice President Thomas A. Hendricks — and the $5 National Bank notes of Series 1882 bearing the portrait of assassinated President James A. Garfield as being commemorative in theme.

The color green is so traditional with our paper money that we refer to U.S. paper currency as "greenbacks." Has the United States ever printed paper money in any other color?

More times than you might suppose. The 1878-1880 series of large-size Silver Certificates had their backs printed with black ink. Paper tinted yellow was used to print the 1870-1884 issues of National Gold Bank notes. Gold Certificates were printed with brilliant golden-orange backs to symbolize the gold coins they represented. Series 1882 National Bank notes have brown backs. Fractional Currency issues of the Civil War period were printed in various colors.

I have heard, but find it difficult to believe, that the United States has issued paper money that was not only circulating legal tender but also bore interest. Is this true?

A number of profit inducements were devised by the Treasury Department in the mid-19th century to overcome America's traditional distrust of paper money. First Issue 1862 Legal Tender Notes could be exchanged for U.S. 6 per cent bonds. An act of 1863 authorized an issue of Interest Bearing Notes that bore interest at the rate of 5 per cent for one or two years or 7.3 per cent for three years. Three Year notes had coupons attached that could be used for collecting the interest semiannually. The same act authorized Compound Interest Treasury Notes that bore interest at 6 per cent compounded semiannually but payable only at maturity. An act of 1879 authorized $10 Refunding Certificates that bore interest indefinitely at the rate of 4 per cent annually. Interest payment wasn't terminated until 1907, when the interest on them amounted to $11.30, giving the $10 Refunding Certificates a redemption value of $21.30. All of these interest-bearing notes could also be used as circulating legal tender.

The people were so distrustful of the first issue of United States paper money, the Demand Notes of 1861, that they discounted them as much as 65 per cent. Yet within a decade they were routinely accepting paper money at face value. How do you account for the change of attitude?

The foundation for confidence in paper money was established by the National Banking Act of February 25, 1863, which required banks to secure their bank note issues with U.S. Government bonds deposited with the Treasurer of the United States.

Is it true that the first issue of government stamp money, the only one of the five issues to be called Postage Currency, was actually illegal?

That is probably true. Rather than being strictly "postage and other stamps of the United States," and despite being "receivable for postage stamps at any U.S. post office," Postage Currency took the form of reproductions of postage stamps on paper carrying the promise of the government that it could be exchanged for United States notes, thereby acquiring the attributes of a promissory note, which was not the intent of Congress.

There are error coins and error bank notes. Are there also error specimens of Fractional Currency?

Through an engraver's oversight, the word CENTS does not appear on the 10-cent denomination of the third issue of Fractional Currency.

I have a specimen of Fractional Currency printed on paper watermarked "C.S." What does this indicate?

Some specimen notes of the second and third issues of Fractional Currency were printed on paper made in Europe for the printing of Confederate Currency, and seized as contraband in 1862 from the *Bermuda,* a captured blockade-runner. This paper was watermarked "C.S.A." (Confederate States of America) in block letters. Fractional Currency notes printed on this paper bear either the letters "C.S." or "S.A."

Can you tell me what a "Lazy 2" bank note is?

"Lazy 2" is a name collectors have given to the $2 note of First Issue or "Original Series" National Bank notes. The name refers to the large numeral 2 shown reclining on its side on the face of the note. Similar large numerals can also be found on obsolete notes.

I have noticed that all National Bank notes bear a full date. Is this the date the note was issued?

The exact significance of the date on a National Bank note has not been determined. It is not the date the note was issued. Nor is it necessarily the date the issuing bank was chartered; the date is usually later, but occasionally earlier, than the charter date of the bank.

When was paper with silk threads first used as a deterrent to counterfeiting?

Paper with silk threads was first used in printing the series of 1869 Legal Tender notes. A warning against counterfeiting was also printed on the back of these notes.

The Mint Act of April 2, 1792, provided that the figure of an eagle appear upon the reverse of all gold and silver coins. When did the eagle make its first appearance on paper money of the United States?

The American Eagle first appeared on U.S. paper currency on the face of the series 1862 Legal Tender $100 note.

My scoutmaster says that people used postage stamps for money during the Civil War. Was this legal, and how did they carry the fragile bits of gummed paper?

Stamps were a legal medium of exchange in amounts up to $5 after July 17, 1862. Until they were replaced by Postage and Fractional Currency, some issues of which bore reproductions of U.S. postage stamps, stamps were prepared for use as currency by pasting them on one half of a folded sheet of paper, by putting them in small envelopes, and by displaying them in small, round brass holders with mica fronts through which the stamps could be viewed.

Introduced in 1862 as an emergency circulation medium, encased postage stamps soon were replaced by fractional currency. The brass holders were always embossed with advertising messages.

Why are the ends of Fractional Currency notes of the Fourth and Fifth Issues tinted blue and violet?

For the same reason that a surcharge was overprinted on the face and back of notes of the second and third issues, to make the work of counterfeiters more difficult.

The third issue of Fractional Currency is the only one of the five issues to include a 3-cent note. Why was it necessary?

The 3-cent note was required to facilitate purchase of the first class 3-cent postage stamp, a role the silver 3-cent piece was no longer able to perform due to the hoarding of specie.

Why did nearly 100 years pass between the time when the motto "In God We Trust" was incorporated into the nation's coin designs and it's adoption on paper money commencing with the 1957 series?

That's not a question that can be answered with certainty. Initially, the motto just "happened" onto our coins, first with it's incorporation of the new two-cent piece introduced in 1864, at which time religious sentiment had been heightened as a result of the Civil War. It was also incorporated into the design of the new nickel introduced in 1866 — from 1883 through 1912, when the Liberty nickel was current, the motto was missing from the nickel — at which time it was also adapted to the existing silver coinages in the quarter through dollar denominations, along with the gold half eagles, eagles and double eagles.

When President Theodore Roosevelt in 1907 directed a redesign of the nation's gold coinage, the new eagle and double eagle designs by Augustus Saint-Gaudens were introduced without the motto. Saint-Gaudens had, with the support of the President, who personally objected to the use of the Deity's name on coins, eliminated this feature from his designs in the essence of artistic simplicity and expression. Congress acted in 1908 to override his objections, requiring that all future U.S. coin issues carry the motto. It was to first appear on the new Lincoln cent in 1909, but did not make it's first appearance on the dime until Weinman's new winged Liberty head design was introduced in 1916.

Another 47 years passed before Congress acted, and President Eisenhower on July 11, 1955, signed into law regulations requiring that the motto be featured on the nation's paper money, and in the interim it was never incorporated as a basic design element. It did appear as an incidental element of currency design on one occasion, however, that being on the 1886 series five dollar Silver Certificate issue. The reverse of that design featured representations of five Morgan silver dollars, four of the pieces being reverses displaying the motto.

Continental Currency and Broken Bank Notes

What is meant by the term "shinplaster"?

The American War for Independence was a time of great ideals and small preparations. There was grand talk of inalienable rights, and a dearth of supplies for the quartermaster. When a soldier bled, he stanched the flow with a plaster of papers. When his stocking wore out and his boots chafed his ankles, he wrapped his feet with a protective layer of paper. These papers acquired the name of "shinplasters" from the second use. Once used for either purpose, they were as worthless as a struck match.

The term has since been applied to Continental currency, U.S. Fractional currency and sometimes state bank notes, particularly when their value was questionable.

You often hear the phrase, "scarce as a $3 bill." Did such a piece of money ever exist?

Yes, as did a $4 and $8 bill, and a host of other odd denominations. They were all issued before the adoption of a federal currency in 1861. Between 1837 and 1857, states, banks, savings institutions and various other organizations issued paper notes in such seemingly odd denominations as 6¼ ¢, 12½ ¢, $1.25, $1.50, $1.75 and $2.50. In reality, the denominations were logical and of benefit to everyday commerce at a time when United States and Spanish coins circulated concurrently, and people were accustomed to goods priced in terms of the Spanish bit (12½ ¢) and its fractions and multiples.

These notes are no longer legal tender, but are prized by collectors, with many issues being excessively rare and very valuable.

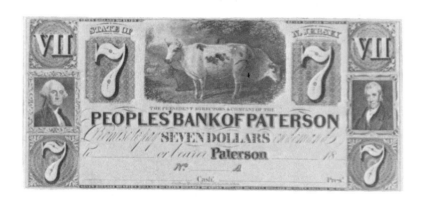

Many odd denominations can be found among the broken bank notes, a name attached to them because most of the private banks did not redeem their issues.

What does the term "broken bank notes" mean?

The present system of United States paper money began with the Civil War. Prior to 1861, the chief form of paper currency were notes issued by banks operating under charters from the states. These notes were generally backed only by a pledge of stock, a backing that merely reflected the anticipation that the institution would endure and prosper. Inevitably, many such banks were unable to withstand the effects of mismanagement, under-financing or financial panic, and literally "went broke," and were unable to redeem their notes. Thus the term, "broken bank notes."

Why is it that some types of Colonial Currency once thought to be quite scarce are now encountered with greater frequency?

Occasionally surplus notes or duplicates, or entire collections, of Colonial Currency are put on the market by museums and State Archives. In recent years, many Connecticut issues once thought to be rare were made available to collectors in this manner.

Is there any way of determining how many broken bank notes were issued?

The gigantic task of cataloging broken bank notes, the largest series of U.S. paper money, has been undertaken by the Society of Paper Money Collectors. Their useful work is far from complete. It has been speculated that more than 30,000 varieties of this type note were issued by 1,600 banks in 34 different states between 1790 and 1865.

Recently at a state coin convention I saw an exhibit consisting of a number of $1.75 bank notes. How do you account for this unusual denomination?

The notes were probably broken bank notes, which exist in such unusual denominations as $1.75, $2.50, $3, $4, $6, $7, $8, $9, $12, $13 and even more exotic units of value. The $1.75 note was directly related to the piece of eight reales which was legal tender in the United States until 1857. The piece of eight was divided into eight 12½-cent "bits." Fourteen bits were exactly equal to $1.75.

When did the national identification "United States" first appear on a government issue of paper money?

When first issued in May of 1775, Continental Currency bore the title "The United Colonies." That identification was continued subsequent to the Declaration of Independence until May 1777, when the title was changed to read "The United States." The title was enlarged to "The United States of North America" on the last issue of Continental Currency, dated January 14, 1779.

I've been told that the term "not worth a Continental" was derived from money. Is this correct?

Yes. The first type of money issued by the Continental Congress, the first U.S. central government, was a form of paper money known as Continental Currency. In theory it was redeemable in Spanish milled dollars, but as the Continental Congress had no specie to back the note emissions it authorized, and no practical authority to implement and inforce its pronouncements, the paper rapidly inflated to the point of no meaningful value; in 1780, 27,733½ Continental Dollars were required to purchase ten head of cattle valued at 200 Spanish silver dollars. The Continental Currency was rejected by the people and never redeemed by the government; because of it, "not worth a Continental" came to denote the complete absence of value.

Continental Currency such as this piece lost its value quickly, giving rise to the expression, "Not worth a Continental."

United States Medals

I have an eight-sided silver piece on the obverse of which is a mining complex identified as "Pikes Peak Silver Mine," and the legend, "In the people we trust. A commodity will give in exchange merchandise at . . ." The reverse carries the legend, "Jos. Leshers Referendum Souvenir Medal, Price $1.00," and a serial number. For what purpose was this item intended?

The piece is a token known as the "Lesher Referendum Dollar" because they were to be referred to the people for acceptance or rejection. They were coined by Joseph Lesher in 1900 and 1901 at Victor, Colorado, in five basic varieties, each of which contained an ounce of coin silver. It is believed the issue was intended to help open idle silver mines.

They were distributed by interested merchants who redeemed them in merchandise. All bear a serial number, and the 1901 issue had a blank space at bottom of obverse for imprinting the names of the merchants who bought and distributed them.

Government officials stopped all coinage of the pieces and seized the dies. Surviving specimens are rare and quite valuable.

I have a silver coin the same size as a U.S. silver dollar, and it has a portrait on the obverse along with the name Hendrik Hudson and the date 1609. The reverse shows a ship under full sail, with the lettering "Nieuw Amsterdam. MCMIX," and "1 Daaler." From what country did this coin originate?

What you have is neither a coin nor foreign. It is a private medal of Thomas L. Elder, struck and issued in the United States in 1909 to commemorate the exploration of the Hudson River by Henry Hudson in 1609. In addition to silver, the dollar-size medal was also struck in aluminum; a variety the size of the U.S. gold dollar was struck in several metals. The portrait on the obverse is that of the English captain Henry Hudson, who was commissioned by the Dutch to find a passage to the Indies by way of the North Pole. The ship on reverse is the Halve Maen.

This particular medal falls within a quaint class of numismatic items known as "So-Called Dollars." This category includes U.S. medals commemorating historical events of national and regional significance, and issues of a monetary nature issued from 1826 through 1961. In order to qualify, a piece must generally fall within the size range of 1¼ to 1¾ inches.

I have seen a number of large silver medals, the size of a silver dollar or larger, dated 1896. They all seem to have one of two phrases inscribed on them, "16 to 1 NIT" or "Free Silver." What are these pieces?

The medals, known as "Bryan Dollars," are campaign pieces associated with the 1896 and 1900 Presidential campaigns of William Jennings Bryan as nominee of the Democratic party and chief spokesman for the advocates of bimetallism at a ratio of 16 to 1 with free and unlimited coinage of silver.

Many were of a satirical nature, deprecating a gold standard, tight money, and the debased silver dollar; and bearing such mottos as, IN GOD WE TRUST FOR THE OTHER 53 CENTS, a pointed reference to the United States silver dollar which contained but 47 cents worth of silver. The symbol "16 to 1 NIT" states the desired ratio of silver to gold, with NIT ("Not in Trust") indicating that the supporters of Bryan did not put their trust in a dollar valued in excess of its bullion worth. This was further emphasized by the huge size of some of the pieces which strikingly illustrated what a dollar's worth of silver really looked like.

Bryan Dollars are quite scarce today, and because of their size, silver content, nostalgic appeal and historical significance command substantial premiums.

Are the designs on the so-called "Olympic" medals struck for public sale the same as on those awarded to the victorious athletes? Is the large "gold" medal awarded to those who place first in their competition really gold?

The designs utilized on the official Olympic award medals are not made available to the general public. The gold medal is actually .925 fine (sterling) silver gilded with "at least 6 grams of the purest gold." The second place medal is .925 fine silver, and the third place medal is bronze. These standards were set in 1928, when it was also established that the medals should be no smaller than 50mm in diameter and 3mm thick. The winter and summer Olympic medals are of different design.

Are the medals that pour from the presses of the private mints in a seemingly endless stream good investment items?

They haven't proven to be, but they are seldom purchased for that purpose. The appeal of medals derives from artistic, historical or nostalgic considerations. Many of the silver issues and series promoted from the mid-1960s through late 70s were melted down for their bullion value when the silver price balooned in the early 80s, however, providing their purchasers with substantial profits. The quantities of some issues and series that survive are probably quite unlimited.

What is the difference between a medallion, a medal and a medalet?

All three can be issued to commemorate a person or event, or awarded for excellence or achievement. The difference is a matter of size, and that distinction isn't very finely drawn. Generally, a medallion is considered to be a medal greater than three inches in diameter. A medalet is a medal the size of a half dollar (1-3/16 inches) or smaller.

I am, of course, familiar with proof coins. Are medals also produced in proof condition?

The majority of the medals being produced today by the better private mints are struck in proof condition. Their manufacture involves highly polished planchets and dies, and two or more strikings to produce sharpness of detail and high relief. As an experiment in collector reception, the United States Mint struck a miniature Jimmy Carter presidential medal in proof for sale at the 1977 ANA convention in Atlanta, Georgia.

During World War II, I was awarded the Distinguished Service Medal by the Army, but actual presentation of the medal never took place. Is it possible for me to obtain my medal at this late date?

You can apply for your medal to the Army Records Center, 9700 Page Blvd., St. Louis, Missouri 63132. The Air Force Records Center and the Naval Records Center can also be contacted at the same address. The Marine Corps can be contacted at Arlington Annex, Washington, D.C. 20308, and the Coast Guard Commandant at Washington, D.C. 20591. Proof of service and your old military number must accompany your application. The delayed awards service applies only to service medals or decorations. Rifle, pistol or combat infantry badges are not included.

I have been told that it is possible to purchase commemorative medals from the U.S. Mint. Can you furnish details?

About 200 different historically attuned medals dating from Revolutionary War days to the present are stocked for sale by the Mint. They are bronze, from 11/16 of an inch to 3 inches in diameter. A complete listing may be obtained from the United States Mint, 55 Mint St., San Francisco, CA 94175.

Is the striking of commemorative medals as active an enterprise as it was ten years ago?

It has been estimated that from the mid-1960s to the late 70s, more commemorative medals were struck to commemorate a greater variety of events than were struck during the previous century.

I understand that the United States Government issues national medals. When did the practice begin?

As early as the Revolutionary War, the United States Government began authorizing the striking of medals for presentation to outstanding military heroes. The first of these medals were made at the French Mint, principally under the direction of Thomas Jefferson, then United States Ambassador to the Court of France. With the exception of the medal awarded to Major Henry ("Light Horse Harry") Lee for the Battle of Paulus Hook, all of the Revolutionary medals were executed in Paris. Although positive proof is lacking, and is likely to remain so, it is believed that the Lee medal, for which Joseph Wright engraved the dies, was struck at the Philadelphia Mint between 1792 and 1796. Bronze copies of the Revolutionary medals were made available to the public, starting in the 1860's.

I have heard that the Mint used "pure" gold and silver when striking national medals. Is this true?

It is, with a few exceptions. As many as 80 blows were required to bring up the relief when medals were struck on the old screw press. Pure gold and silver, being softer than alloys, extended the working life of dies. On a few occasions, .900 fine gold or silver was used. In at least one instance, the Mecklenburg Centennial, the medal was struck on regular-issue half dollar planchets.

Collectors of the copper or bronze medals of the U.S. Mint refer to them as "copper-bronzed," "mahogany," "dark chocolate," or "late bronze." Can you sort these terms out for me?

Until about 1901, the Mint struck medals of copper and then "bronzed" them by heat and/or chemical treatment. "Copper-bronzed" medals made from about 1825 to about 1891 are distinguished by a proof surface and a color ranging from light red to dark brown. Collectors call them "mahogany finish" medals. From about 1891 to about 1901, "copper-bronzed" medals have a dull surface and a dark brown color. They are called "dark chocolate" medals. From about 1901, the Mint has employed a true bronze alloy (.950 copper, .050 tin and zinc). After being struck, the bronze medals are sandblasted. Medals made by this process are known to collectors as "late bronze" or "yellow bronze" specimens.

Has the Mint ever struck medals in any metal other than gold, silver, copper and bronze?

A very few were struck in nickel, aluminum, white metal, copper-nickel, goloid, brass and lead. Those in lead are almost certainly die trials.

I once read somewhere that the U.S. Mint struck a series of medals that were strictly commemorative in nature. When was this, and are the medals still available?

The Mint struck a most interesting series of commemorative medals prior to 1892, when the minting of commemorative coins began. The quality of workmanship revealed by many of them can be inferred from the names of some of the engravers: John Reich, Charles and William Barber, Augustin Dupre, George Morgan, Anthony Paquet and James Longacre. These medals were struck in a variety of metals (copper, bronze, gold, and silver, white-metal, goloid, aluminum), and range in size from a demure 19mm to a generous 76mm. While some were issued simply to cash in on the hour's enthusiasm for a particular person or event, many are of lasting national significance. A few of the commemorated events plucked at random from the list reveal the bemusing diversity of theme: U.S. Centennial, Emancipation Proclamation, Lexington Centennial, Valley Forge Centennial, Schuylkill Navy, National Convention of Cattlemen, the Chicago Fire and The Mighty Dollar.

Several of these Mint commemorative medals are still available for sale to the public. Most of the pre-1892 commemorative medals are relatively scarce and provide the collector with a demanding challenge.

Is it true that the Mint once struck museum tokens and awards for dog shows?

Yes, and also for kennel clubs, bicycle clubs, horse shows, athletic associations, fire companies, music societies and many other clubs and organizations. These pieces were struck in gold, silver and/or copper during the latter half of the 19th century, to the order of private individuals and club officials. The mintage of most pieces was quite small, in some instances less than a dozen examples were delivered. The "museum tokens" were made for the Charles Wilson Peale Museum in Philadelphia. They have been popular with collectors for more than a century, possibly because of the belief that they were engraved by Christian Gobrecht.

My grandfather had a school medal he always claimed was made by the U.S. Mint. Is this possible?

From about 1831 to comparatively recent times, the Mint struck medals for various educational institutions which purchased them for use as scholastic achievement awards, and in at least one instance for "punctuality and deportment." Many were still being struck after 1900. The practice was discontinued about 1947, when the last of the Franklin medals were struck for the Boston schools.

When did the U.S. Mint initiate the practice of striking copies of national medals specifically for sale to the general public?

In January 1861, sixteen prominent numismatists, including inventor Samuel F. B. Morse, signed a letter addressed to Treasury Secretary John A. Dix in which they suggested that copies of national medals be struck for public sale. The secretary gave his assent on February 14 of that year.

How many so-called "official" Bicentennial medals were issued during 1975-1976?

Official Bicentennial medals received their authority through Congress by the participation of their issuers in the medal program of the American Revolution Bicentennial Administration (ARBA). Forty-eight of the states issued a Bicentennial medal bearing the ARBA label, as did many cities. Mississippi and West Virginia did not participate in the state medal program. It has been estimated that official Bicentennial Commissions issued at least 106 medals.

Is it true that when the Mint first offered copies of national medals to the public, the large copper-bronzed pieces cost a mere $1.50?

Yes, but it is equally true that in 1861 the average daily wage was less than two dollars.

What medals were most popular with collectors before those of the Bicentennial year?

Space medals, particularly those relevant to the lunar voyages, and medals honoring the memory of former President John F. Kenndy were, and still are, enthusiastically collected.

What are Masonic "Mark Pennies," and are they still being made?

Originally, Masonic Mark Pennies were copper or bronze medal-like pieces bearing the identity and location of the issuing lodge, the Masonic symbols, and the private "mark" of the new member to whom the penny was given. The piece served to identify the member when presented at the issuing or other Masonic lodges. Today, Mark Pennies are produced principally as anniversary commemoratives for exchange between lodges and sale to members and non-members alike. During the last half of the 19th century, a number of Masonic lodges, including the New York Masonic Temple and St. John's Commandery in Philadelphia, had their Mark Pennies struck by the U.S. Mint.

How are elongated coins classified? Are they medals or still coins?

I have never heard them referred to as other than Elongated Coins. If a choice has to be made between coins and medals, they can only be regarded as commemorative medals inasmuch as the die impressions that made them coins has been all but obliterated by the elongating process.

Is it possible to obtain bronze copies of any medal the Mint has ever struck?

No, only of a select few hundred considered to be of national interest. The Mint began striking medals about 1800, and for many years actively sought private orders. The customer would either have the dies for his medal engraved by a private artist, or would hire a Mint engraver to prepare them on his own time. In either case, the dies belonged to the customer, and were not deposited in the Mint die collection. Consequently, the dies for literally thousands of private medals struck by the U.S. Mint no longer exist.

Are the copies of Indian peace medals available from the Mint today exact copies of those formerly presented to Indian chiefs?

They differ in size and metal, but with a few exceptions the designs are authentic. The Indian peace medal issued under Washington's administration consisted of two hand-engraved silver plates bound together with a silver band. Its design bore no resemblance to the Washington peace or presidential medal available today. No medals for Indians were made during the administrations of John Adams and William Henry Harrison. They were designed and struck later to complete the presidential series.

United States Tokens

I have a coin which has a head similar to the one on the old large United States cents, along with the date 1837. On the reverse is some lettering which reads, "Millions for defense, not one cent for tribute." What do I have?

You have an example of the privately issued necessity money of 1833-1844 known as "Hard Times Tokens." They are generally struck in copper, were of the size of the large cent, and are of two general groups: political tokens and tradesmen's cards. Although they circulated as cents during a time of severe financial panic characterized by a lack of circulating coin caused by the hoarding of hard money, many bore a monetary disclaimer cleverly incorporated in patriotic slogans, such as "Millions for defense, NOT ONE CENT for tribute."

The theme of the political tokens centers upon Jackson's refusal to renew the charter of the Bank of the United States; many of the designs are strongly satirical, ridiculing Jackson's sketchy formal education, mule-like stubbornness, and pretensions in office.

I recently came across a coin about the size of a current one-cent piece which I cannot identify. The obverse depicts a perched eagle and the date 1837, while on the reverse are the words "Feuchtwanger's Composition," in addition to "One Cent." What is this?

The coin is commonly called a Feuchtwanger Cent. Dr. Lewis Feuchtwanger, a German-born chemist, perfected a metal which was really a variety of German silver, consisting of nickel, copper and some zinc. In 1837 he petitioned the U.S. government to consider using his metal as a substitute for copper in coinage, and struck a number of one-cent and three-cent trial pieces in the design you describe. Many tokens of the Hard Times period, including a number of his own Store Cards, were issued in Feuchtwanger's metal.

Dr. Feuchtwanger was the first to suggest a small cent and a three-cent piece, coins the government later adopted.

I have a coin which depicts on the obverse a bird rising from flames, and lettering which reads, "Substitute for Shin Plasters, Nov., 1837." On the reverse is some wording which reads, "Specie Payments Suspended, May, Tenth, 1837." What is this item?

This is another of the political-motif Hard Times Tokens. The symbolism of a Phoenix bird rising from the flames is intended to suggest that the paper money of the time had become fit only to be burned; but that with its destruction, hard money would pump new life into the moribund economy.

The inspiration for the theme was derived from a convention of leading bankers who met in New York and decided that suspended specie payments could be resumed on May 10, 1838.

Hard Times Tokens

I have a coin which is dated 1863, has an Indian head on the obverse, and is the same size as our current one-cent piece, but on the reverse it states, "Not One Cent." Can you tell me what kind of a coin this is?

Your "coin" quite possibly served as such, but is actually a privately issued patriotic Civil War token. These were issued by merchants during a severe coin shortage of Civil War days to provide a small coin for everyday transactions. Many were imitations of the Indian Head cent which had at the time only recently been introduced into circulation; others bore such traditional devices as the Liberty Head, U.S. shield, flags, eagles, and portraits of the Founding Fathers. Most were made of copper; other compositions were brass, lead, zinc, nickel and copper-nickel. They were finally outlawed by Act of Congress in 1864.

These tokens generally bore a device symbolic of patriotism, or a patriotic slogan, such as "The Union Must And Shall Be Preserved." The most familiar of this type is the famous "Dix cent." On Jan. 29, 1861, Secretary of the Treasury John Adams Dix ended a letter of instruction to a Lieut. Caldwell with the unequivocal charge, "If anyone attempts to haul down the American flag, shoot him on the spot." Inevitably, the slogan ended up on Civil War tokens, but due to an engraver's error some examples read, "... shoot him on the SPOOT."

Two Civil War tokens. Most were issued by merchants who had to keep some form of small change circulating or go out of business.

I have a round copper disc which has an Indian Head with 13 stars and the date 1863 on one side, and on the other some lettering which reads, "Pekin Tea Store, No. 50 St. Clair St., Pittsburgh." What is this item?

The item you have is a one-cent trade token known as a Civil War Store Card or Merchants Token. These differ from the Civil War Patriotic Tokens in bearing an advertisement of the issuing merchant. They were issued by merchants in almost 300 towns in 23 states, mostly in the North, with a few issues from the border states. It is estimated that the combined minting of Civil War Patriotic Tokens and Store Cards comprised more than 50,000,000 pieces in about 10,000 varieties.

The particular token you have is one of nearly 200 different Civil War Store Cards issued by some 30 firms in Western Pennsylvania, mostly in Pittsburgh or old Allegheny.

In my collection is a small coin which looks like gold and is about the size of a U.S. $2-1/2 gold piece. It has an odd-looking Liberty head on the obverse, along with the legend "Republica Argentina Libertad." On the reverse is an eagle and the legend, "United States of America 2-1/2 D." Is this possibly a pattern for a proposed international coinage?

It is not a pattern, but rather a common numismatic item known as "American Game Counters" or "Spiel Marken." These were commonly employed as stakes or markers in games of chance during the mid-1800s, much as poker chips are used today.

Many were made in imitation of U.S. coins; other utilized Latin American designs in conjunction with U.S. designs. The majority were manufactured in the private mints of Germany, and in Birmingham, England. The scarcer varieties are highly valued, but most issues are relatively common. Their metallic composition is generally gilded bronze or brass, not gold.

I have a token which has on both sides the elephant depicted on the famous American Colonial elephant tokens. On one side is the legend, "Only 10 Struck." Is this a modern fantasy piece?

Your token is one of the prestigious Colonial copies struck in the 1860s by J.A. Bolen. Ten were struck with the legend, and two without.

Copies were made of a great variety of Colonial coins during the middle of the 19th century and the opening years of the 20th century to provide facsimiles of rare issues that would otherwise be unobtainable. Time has given them a status denied current copies, which are not generally recognized as meaningful collector items.

I have an item which has me completely puzzled. On one side it has the words, "Streator Yellow Bus Co.," and on the other side, "Good For One Fare." The lettering is around the outside, in the center are three holes, which leave what looks like a "Y" suspended in the center. In the background are some intricately drawn lines. The piece is white and about the size of a nickel. Can you tell me what purpose this piece served?

Your puzzle is a "Transportation" or "Vecturist" token. They were issued for fares for any mode of transportation or associated facility, such as, toll gates, bridges, inclined planes, boats, ferries, stage coaches, horse cars, street cars, buses and trains. Their origin is obscure, but it is known that in 18th century England they took the form of passes for use of the King's Roads. They were first employed in this country in 1790, and were extremely popular in the last half of the 19th century. The pierced variety came into use early in this century, and is quite prevalent today.

I have what is identified as a "Colorado Retail Sales Tax Token." It also carries the figure "2" and has a cross-shaped area removed from the center. It is about the size of a nickel, and struck in aluminum. When was it used?

Sales Tax Tokens were issued by various states in the mid-1930s to facilitate the payment of the sales tax before the amount due was calculated in even cents. The piece you mention was valued at two mills.

They were round, square, rectangular in shape; with and without center holes; were made of metal, fiber or plastic; and were frequently distinguished by a color code, such as black, white, green and red.

From left: Transportation token, sales tax token and merchants token, or store card.

*I have a brass coin which on one side has, EL-RUS, BAR, IOLA, WISC.,
and on the other, 10¢ IN TRADE. It looks real old. What was it used for, and
what is it worth?*

You have what is known as a "Store Card" or "Merchant's Token." They
have been issued by merchants, tavern owners, clubs, restaurants, gaming
houses, "company stores" of coaltowns, etc., from the post-Colonial era to the
present for advertising or trade purposes, and are redeemable to stated
amount in trade at the issuing establishment. The category includes such historic issues as Hard Times Tokens, Civil War Tokens, and the modern
depression issues.

Collectors particularly value the elaborately designed Store Cards of the
first half of the 19th century, and the later issues that feature intricate geometric patterns; some of these command significant premiums. The piece you
describe would appear to be of the mid 1900s, and these are not especially
valuable.

*I have a piece of paper which somewhat resembles a dollar bill. It is titled,
"One Dollar Scrip Note," and was issued the 6th day of March, 1933, by the
Industrial Loan and Investment Co. of Fort Wayne, Indiana. What is the
nature of this note?*

This note is one of an extensive issue of "Depression Scrip" of the 1930s. It
was issued during the bank holiday proclaimed by President Roosevelt in
March of 1933, when no other medium of exchange was available for everyday
commerce.

The use of Depression Scrip was widespread during that decade of hardship
and tight money; there is scrip from over 500 communities, representing 48
States, the District of Columbia, and the Territory of Hawaii. It was issued by
employers for payroll purpose, by cities in the form of Tax Anticipation
Notes, and by banks, clearing houses, chambers of commerce, individuals,
etc.

Most scrip notes were printed on paper, but some unusual forms were
printed on wood, aluminum, rubber, leather, shells, sheepskin, buckskin,
fishskin. As anticipated, much of the novelty issue was retained for souvenirs,
and never presented for redemption. Most of the paper scrip was redeemed
and destroyed, consequently, many issues are very rare today.

*I have often heard that old expression, "Don't take any wooden nickels,"
and I have seen many of them, and even saved a few. Does anyone collect
them?*

Many collect nothing else. The dictionary defines a wooden nickel as, "A
small wooden disc, souvenir, token, or the like, having a value of five cents, or

no value." Numismatically, it is much more. A wooden nickel can be round or rectangular, and if round, of any size from a nickel or smaller up to a dollar or larger. It can be of any thickness from paper-thin to half an inch. It can be a valid trade token, frequently of commemorative design, usually redeemable as payment on merchandise; or a souvenir of a meeting or celebration; or simply a personal calling or advertising card.

The history of wooden money can be traced back to the Byzantine Empire (395-1435) when an attempt was made to circulate wooden money with little success. Since then, various forms of wooden money have served as a medium of exchange in England, Tibet, China, Africa, Oceania, the South Sea Islands and Canada. The first "official" issue of wooden money in the United States was circulated in 1931 by Tenino, Washington, to provide a medium of exchange during a bank failure which resulted in an acute shortage of circulating money.

I have read that during World War II "colored OPA tokens" were required to purchase canned goods and meats. What did the colors indicate, and are these war-related items collected as "tokens"?

The OPA (Office of Price Administration) "tokens" to which you refer are of a sandwich-type construction, consisting of red or blue outer layers bonded to an uncolored core. They are round, 16.4mm in diameter, 1.4mm thick, and weigh about 4 grains. Strictly speaking, they are not "tokens." They are "points" that were used in conjunction with, rather than in place of, money when purchasing designated food items. A specified number of blue "points" were required to purchase specified amounts of canned fruits and vegetables, fruit juices, soups, baby foods, dried peas, beans and preserves. Red "points" were required to purchase meats, butter, oleo, edible fats and oils, cheese, canned milk and canned fish.

They are collected, usually with emphasis upon the distinguishing alphabet code they bear. There are 54 known alphabetical combinations - 30 blue, 24 red - involving the letters C, H, T, U, V, X, Y and occasionally W and M. The "rare" tokens in the set are the red bearing "MM" and "MV" letter combinations. Ration stamps required for the purchase of gasoline, shoes, clothes, sugar, coffee and other scarce items are also collected.

The fact that copper tokens of private origin circulated freely during the first 80 years of the nation's existence would seem to indicate that they possessed at least an implied legality. On what was it based?

The legal status of private copper tokens prior to the Law of June 8, 1864, which provided for fines of up to $5,000 and 10 years at hard labor for the issuing of a private coinage of any kind, has never been clarified. An act of 1792, made it a misdemeanor punishable by a $10 fine to pay or receive in payment any copper coins other than those of the United States. However, a subsequent act empowered the secretary of the Treasury to annul by proclamation all private and foreign coppers six months after the Mint had issued $50,000 worth of half cents and cents. The required proclamation was never issued, and private tokens continued to be issued and to circulate concurrently with U.S. coppers until 1857.

My brother told me that a token struck in 1796 for use in the United States is still being minted. Can he be right?

In 1792, many French families of wealth and rank fled the French Revolution and established French settlements at Castorville and what is now Carthage, New York. In 1796, Duvivier (designer of some of the early medals of the U.S. Mint) prepared a silver piece known as the "Castorland Half Dollar" either as an honorarium for the Paris Commissioners of Castorland or as a pattern for the coinage of the settlement. A reeded edge and similarity of size and weight to the U.S. half dollar suggests a monetary purpose. This attractive piece can still be ordered from the Paris Mint in gold, silver, bronze or copper, and with matte or brilliant finish.

My mother had a coin or something which she wore as a pendant for many years. She said her grandfather, a sailor, gave it to her. On one side there are crossed sprays, the initials W.P. and the date 1880. There isn't anything on the other side but HALF REAL. What is it?

Your great-grandfather had evidently been to Hawaii. The piece you describe is a plantation token used as small change on the Islands during the latter half of the 19th century. The initials W.P. are those of the Wailuku Plantation.

I have heard that the United States Government (not a private agency) once issued a $10 trade token. If true, when did it happen?

It's true, and it happened in 1935. The aluminum $10 token was part of a series that also included a 1¢, 5¢, 10¢, 25¢, 50¢, $1 and $5 token. The "Bingles," as they were called, were issued for the use of the colonists of the Matanuska Valley Colonization Project in Alaska to provide them with needed federal aid. They were redeemable only at the stores of the Alaska Rural Rehabilitation Corporation (ARRC), and were in use for about six months in 1935, after which they were redeemed for regular U.S. money and destroyed. With the exception of the octagonal one-cent piece, the tokens are round, and of the same size as the corresponding U.S. coin.

Canadian Coins and Currency

I have a large Canadian coin or token that bears the denomination one penny. Also, the legend on this coin states that it is a bank token of Upper Canada. Just what is Upper Canada, and what does this token represent?

Ontario was largely founded by the immigration of United Empire Loyalists into Canada after the Declaration of Independence of the United States. The Constitutional Acts adopted by England in 1792 divided it into two separate provinces called Upper Canada, chiefly English-speaking, and Lower Canada, the French stronghold. Upper Canada consisted of the southern part of present Ontario, and Lower Canada can be identified with Quebec.

The tokens of this instance, known as the St. George tokens, were an authorized issue of the Bank of Upper Canada. They were issued in denominations of penny and halfpenny in the years 1850, 52, 54 and 57.

How many mints are there in Canada, and do they have mint marks?

The Royal Canadian Mint at Ottawa, established in 1908, was the sole Canadian minting facility until mid-summer of 1975, when a large, modern facility at Winnipeg began production. Eventually, the Manitoba plant was expected to handle manufacture of coins for circulation, freeing the Ottawa facility for production of special collector items. The Canadian C mint mark has appeared only on gold sovereigns minted for the British Empire and on certain Newfoundland coins struck before Newfoundland became a province of Canada.

Tokens played a prominent role in the commerce of early Canada. Two of the most common were the penny and half-penny tokens issued in the 1850s by the Bank of Upper Canada.

Does the obverse of Canadian coins always bear the portrait of the ruling monarch of the British Empire?

It isn't mandatory, but coins of the British colonies and associated Commonwealth nations frequently bear the portrait of the ruling British monarch.

I have a Canadian large cent that has on "H" on its reverse. Of what significance is this letter?

The "H" stands for Heaton, and is the mint mark of a private mint located in Birmingham, England, to which the Royal Mint subcontracts. Most of the early coins of Canada were struck at the Tower Mint in London, and bear no mint mark.

Has the Royal Canadian Mint at Ottawa ever placed any type of mint mark on any of the coins it has produced for Canada?

The Ottawa Mint has at no time placed any type of mint mark on any of the coins struck specifically for domestic use in Canada. However, the Royal Canadian Mint has minted gold sovereigns for the British Empire, and has placed the distinguishing mint mark C on the reverse of these coins to indicate that they were struck at Ottawa.

I have a coin dated 1941 that bears the word "Newfoundland." I always thought that Newfoundland was a part of Canada. Can you explain this dilemma?

Newfoundland did not become a province of the Dominion of Canada until April 1, 1949. Prior to this time, Newfoundland had its own coins. The Newfoundland coinage was struck at London, Birmingham and Ottawa. The Tower Mint coins (London) have no mint mark, the Birmingham coins have the characteristic Heaton H, and those produced at Ottawa bear the Canadian mint mark C.

I have noticed that Canada, the United States, and Newfoundland have all issued 20¢ coins at one time or another. Can you shed any light on why this coin ever came into being and why it was never accepted?

A 20-cent piece is a logical development of a decimal system of coinage; a 25-cent piece is an anomaly. However, the pre-national currency experience of both the United States and Canada was predominantly influenced by the Spanish dollar and its eight subdivisions, of which the 2 reales (2 bits) had a value of 25¢. It should be remembered that the Spanish dollar and its minor coins were legal tender in the United States until 1857, and that U.S. coins circulated freely in Canada before that country established a monetary system and a mint. Familiarity with a 25¢ denomination, and the desirability of maximum equivalence in the minor coins of the concurrent currencies, established a use precedent for the quarter which a 20-cent piece was unable to replace in Canada, although Newfoundland circulated the 20-cents denomination from 1865 until 1917.

I have a 1944 Canadian nickel that has a large "V" on the reverse and a border of dots and dashes resembling the Morse code. Can you explain this?

This is the famous Canadian "Victory Nickel" of 1943-45. The torch and V
are symbols of victory. The border of dots and dashes are an inscription in
Morse code, "We Win When We Work Willingly."

*What is meant by the 1947 Maple Leaf cent? All the cents of Canada that
I have in my collection have a maple leaf on the reverse.*

Two issues of the Canadian cent bearing the date 1947 were released: the
regular issue of 1947, and the one with a small maple leaf appearing after the
date which was issued early in 1948. The granting of independence to India
necessitated the removal of ET IND: IMP: from the obverse legend of all
Empire coinage bearing the royal portrait. The 1948 dies incorporating this
change were delayed, and because of a developing coin shortage the 1948
coinage was commenced with 1947 dies. The tiny maple leaf indicates that the
coins so identified were actually struck in 1948.

*What is meant by Arnprior Canadian dollar? I've never seen that word on
any of the Canadian silver dollars that I've examined.*

In December of 1955, after the production of silver dollars had been officially completed for that year, the Royal Canadian Mint struck a special lot of
2000 dollars for a firm in Arnprior, Ontario. These dollars differed from the
previously struck ones in having only one and one-half water lines in front of
the canoe on the reverse of the coin. Collectors refer to them as "Arnpriors."
A small quantity of similar dollars in proof-like condition were issued late in
the year for the 1955 mint sets. A 1950 dollar of like characteristics has bela-
tedly acquired the same identification.

*I have noticed that a lot more attention is devoted to minor die varieties
in collecting late Canadian coins as opposed to U.S. coins of the same
period. Can you explain this?*

In one word: boredom. Canada does not produce mint-marked variety coins, and it produces sufficient quantities of each denomination to enable the collector of Canadian coins to easily acquire the year specimens for his collection. To sustain his interest, the Canadian collector began looking for die varieties and the imperfections inherent to any mass-produced item. Branch mints with their distinctive mint marks and occasional small mintage of a particular denomination, greatly increased the challenge confronting the collector of United States coinage.

What is meant by the "Godless" coins of Canada?

In one year only, 1911, the year George V assumed the reign after the death of Edward VII, the words "Dei Gratia," meaning "By the Grace of God," were omitted from the obverse legend of all Canadian coins. Because of it, they are frequently referred to as the "Graceless" or "Godless" coins. The gold sovereigns bore the abbreviated reference, "D.G."

What is meant by a 1926 near 6 or far 6 nickel?

The description refers to the location of the date numeral 6 in relation to the right-hand maple leaf on the reverse of the coin. On the "near 6" variety, the stem of the 6 almost touches the leaf; on the "far 6" there is a narrow but quite obvious gap. The "far 6" is considered the scarcer of the two varieties.

To what do the expressions "blunt 7" and "pointed 7" refer?

The terms refer to the manner in which the bottom tip of the stem of the date numeral 7 of the 1947 silver dollar is pointed. The point of the "Blunt 7" variety is formed by a single downward diagonal achieving a point where it intersects the left lineament of the stem. The point of the "pointed 7" variety is formed by downward diagonals from each side intersecting at a point in line with center of stem.

Did Canada issue any gold coins prior to introduction of the $100 commemorative series in 1976?

In 1912, 13 and 14, Canada minted a limited quantity of five-dollar and ten-dollar gold coins, of which the coins of 1914 are considered to be the rarest. In 1967, Canada minted a commemorative twenty-dollar gold piece for the specimen sets of commemorative coins marking the 100th anniversary of the Confederation of Canada. These gold coins bear no mint mark, and their reverse design portrays the armorial bearing of Canada.

These Canadian gold coins should not be confused with the gold sovereigns Canada minted for the British Empire from 1908 to 1919, with the exception of 1912 and 1915. These sovereigns are the Edward VII and George V type of Great Britian, and can be distinguished from them only by the Canadian mint mark "C" placed immediately above the date on the reverse of the coin.

What are my chances of finding a 1936 dot cent of Canada?

You probably have a better chance of being elected president. The few known specimens are both uncirculated and unauthenticated. Officially, 678,823 of these dot cents were minted. Two theories have been advanced to account for their virtual non-existence: none were ever released for general circulation, or the dot on the die filled up early in the production run and the distinguishing mark was not raised upon the coins.

The dot coinage of 1936 also included the dime and quarter. The quarters were released to circulation and a limited quantity are available to collectors. But eight specimens are known of the 191,237 dot dimes minted.

The dot was placed at the bottom of the reverse of the 1936 dies to enable them to be used to strike the 1937 George V coinage, until the new dies for the George VI coinage could be prepared.

Did Newfoundland ever issue gold coins?

Newfoundland issued two-dollar gold coins in eight different years during the period of 1865-1888. Curiously, Newfoundland never issued a dollar denomination coin.

To what does the term "devil in the hair" refer, as applied to Canadian paper money?

Devil in Hair

No Devil

It has reference to the 1954 issue of the Bank of Canada, and a resemblance to a devil's face that was noticed in the arrangement of curls behind the left ear of the Queen in her portrait on all denominations of the issue. Due to protests, revisions were made in the engravings to remove this fascinating, but objectionable, feature of the notes.

I have a Canadian coin dated 1942 and another dated 1943 that resemble a regular Canadian nickel. But they are of a bronze-colored material and 12-sided. Is this a coin of regular mintage, or do I have something special?

Because of a shortage of nickel caused by war requirements, the metallic content of the Canadian nickel was changed during 1942 to a bronze-colored alloy of 88 percent copper and 12 percent zinc, called tombac. It was made 12-sided to distinguish it from the bronze cent. It wasn't a success. The coin turned black and it was confused with the cent. During 1944 and 1945 the nickel was made from chrome-plated steel.

As was true in other parts of colonial North America, the void between wampum and real coins was bridged in Canada by a variety of tokens, notes and other forms of exchange. The piece of playing card money, dated 1735, is French. The Hudson's Bay Co. token was good for ½ made beaver (abbreviated NB in error); 1815 Magdalen Island one penny token proclaims "Success to the Fisheries," and the holed Spanish dollar passed for five shillings on Prince Edward Island.

Does Canada mint any proof sets?

The Royal Canadian Mint has regularly offered "uncirculated" or "proof-like six-coin sets sealed in a polyester film packet. These transparent packets contain one coin of each denomination, from the cent through the dollar, struck on selected and specially handled blanks.

In 1971, for the first time since the special Centennial coin sets of 1967, the Royal Canadian Mint offered proof quality coin sets in presentation cases. These sets, containing seven double struck coins, were offered in two versions. The prime set contained two dollar coins to enable the display of each of the individual coin reverses and the uniform obverse and was housed in a satin lined genuine leather case. The alternate set contained two cents instead of two dollars and was housed in a simulated leather case. Either version could be ordered in any quantity from the Royal Canadian Mint. Address: Royal Canadian Mint, P.O. Box 454, Station A, Ottawa, Ontario, Canada K1N 8V5.

I have noted that the Canadian monetary system very closely resembles that of the United States. Was there any direct planning for this between the two countries?

There was no formal agreement. None was necessary. The proximity of the two nations and the common origin and traditions of the majority of their people, a common history of monetary experience with the Spanish dollar, and the tendency of the people of both nations to use each other's money, would have made any other decision irrational.

In view of the fact that the Canadian currency is already designated by various colors, why doesn't the United States add color to the various denominations to correspond with the colors now used in Canada.

The desirability of colored currency has been discussed in the United States for more than a decade. The chief argument for it being that a distinctive color for each denomination would enable it to be more readily identified, and reduce the chance of improper payment or change.

Opponents argue that familiarity with the established designs is sufficient to enable quick identifications without a color code. That, of course, is untrue. Identification is made by the denomination number on the bill, not the design; not one person in five knows whose portrait is on the five-dollar bill.

Whatever the reason, it remains that comparatively few mistakes are made. If a man is smart enough to acquire a thousand dollar bill, he is certainly smart enough to know what he has.

For what were the paper 25¢ notes of Canada used?

In 1870, when the 25¢ fractional notes first appeared, Canadian officials were worried about the large amount of U.S. silver coinage circulating in Canada in default of an adequate supply of regal coins. They were worried because the U.S. dollar was worth but 80¢ in Canada, and the trusting people who accepted the U.S. coins at face value suffered a 20 percent loss when they presented them for conversion to Canadian funds. The decision was made to withdraw the U.S. coins from circulation, and replace them with 25¢ notes until sufficient Canadian coins could be minted.

The notes were intended to be a temporary issue, but the people liked them, particularly for sending small amounts of money through the mail. Further issues were released in 1900 and 1923, and it wasn't until 1935 that the Bank of Canada decided to recall them.

The 1951 Canadian nickel lacks the normal reverse of the beaver, and in its place there is some type of factory with the additional legend "Nickel, 1751-1951." What is the significance of this change of design?

About 75 percent of the 1951 Canadian nickels bear this commemorative reverse which celebrates the 200th anniversary of the isolation of the metal nickel by a Swedish chemist in 1751, and reminds that Canada accounts for 86 percent of the world's nickel production. The factory on the coin was a stylized rendition of a contemporary nickel refinery. A shortage of nickel late in 1951 forced the mint to return to the regular beaver design in chrome-plated steel.

A friend told me that Canada once used playing cards for money. Was he putting me on?

Playing card money was used in the French colonies in Canada for approximately 75 years. Full cards, half cards, quarter cards, and oddly dimensioned clips were utilized.

The first issue, in 1685, was an emergency issue of necessity money. Troop payments from France were delayed. To quell the talk of mutiny, the governor collected all the packs of playing cards in the garrison, wrote an assigned value on the face of the cards and signed them. Both the soldiers and the colonists accepted this do-it-yourself money, and it became so popular that the government was forced to issue it in large quantities.

Playing card money was of convenient size, durable, difficult to forge — and the first paper money issued on the North American continent.

I have a Canadian dollar bill on which an asterisk precedes the serial number. Can you explain this, and does the asterisk increase the value of the note as a collector's item?

The asterisk indicates that the note is a replacement for a defective one removed and destroyed during the printing process. Notes so marked acquire a small additional value because of it.

Is it true that every coin Canada issued in 1967 is a commemorative?

Yes. Canada's philosophy of commemorative distribution differs fundamentally from that employed by the United States. The Canadian commemorative replaces a regular-issue coin for a specified period, usually a year; the

coins are struck in quantity, and released to circulation in the normal manner. In 1967, Canada replaced all of the regular-issue coins (1¢ through $1) with commemoratives to celebrate the 100th anniversary of Canadian Confederation as a nation.

I have a 1967 Canadian dollar bill that has the dates 1867-1967 where the serial numbers would normally appear. Is this dollar related to the 1967 Centennial Celebration?

This dollar bill was issued by the Bank of Canada in Ottawa to commemorate one hundred years of Canadian Confederation as a nation. This particular issue could only be obtained directly from the bank itself, and bears the dates 1867-1967 in place of the regular bill serial numbers. It was issued at the request of and particularly for collectors. A similar 1967 commemorative dollar bill, but with normal serial numbers, as issued for general circulation.

What is the story behind the 1967 $20 gold coin of Canada?

The $20 gold coin was a special issue struck only for inclusion in the Gold Presentation Sets of 1967 coinage commemorating the 100th anniversary of Canadian Confederation as a nation. The seven proof quality coins were encased in a black, morocco leather presentation case, and sold for $40 a set.

This is a coin of many "firsts": the first commemorative gold coin of Canada, the dominion's first gold coin since 1914, the first commemorative gold coin of North America since 1926, the first $20 coin Canada ever minted, and the dominion's largest denomination gold coin. The coin was struck in .900 fine gold, with a bullion value of $20 Canadian and about $18.50 U.S.

American collectors were denied the opportunity to legally purchase this coin at the time of issue. Officials of the U.S. Treasury's Office of Domestic Gold and Silver Operations did not consider the coin to be of sufficient merit for exclusion from the ban then in force which severely limited the ownership of modern gold coins by U.S. citizens. This ban was rescinded at midnight, Dec. 30, 1974. It is a fact, however, that many U.S. collectors had the coins in their possession prior to that time. In fact, many purchased them at the time of issue and placed them in bank safe deposit boxes in Canada, which action was also technically unlawful.

Mexican Coins and Currency

What did the natives use for exchange before the arrival of the Spanish?

In a slave-owning culture such as the Aztec Empire, slaves constituted the wealth of the owner and provided the standard, if not the unit, of value. There may have been a need for small change in such communities, but it existed only as a convenient subdivision of the real wealth. Consequently, there was a scarcity of primitive money in Mexico.

The highest Aztec monetary unit was a sack containing about 24,000 cocoa beans. Interestingly, the cocoa-bean money was debased, by being hollowed out and repacked with dirt; and counterfeited with imitation beans of varnished clay. Pieces of cotton cloth, stone beads and colored shells were also employed as a low-level medium of exchange. Extremely expensive purchases were made with transparent duck quills packed with flakes of gold.

Some authorities cite a small copper axe (sometimes called a hoe or hide scraper) as a form of token money. Others believe the axe money was introduced 25 years after the conquest to facilitate trade between the Spaniards and Indians in lieu of sufficient small Spanish coins.

Did the Spaniards bring their own coins to the New World, did they use the native exchange media, or did they begin making coins as soon as they arrived?

Spain never made a serious attempt to supply New Spain (Mexico) with coinage from the Old World. At the beginning there was no need of it; the conquistadores came as looters, not traders. When developing trade created a need for coinage, it was considered more convenient, cheaper, and safer (in view of the action of privateers) to coin the silver at its source. The first mint in the New World was established at Mexico City in 1535, and coined one quarter, one half, one, two and four real pieces. Two and four copper maravedies were also coined, but were not accepted by the natives, who also refused the fractional silver reales because of their smallness.

The consequent shortage of coins of sufficiently low denomination for trading with the impoverished natives forced the Spaniards to utilize native currencies, principally the copper hoe and cocoa bean. According to a Spanish document of 1548, four new hoes were equal in value to five Spanish reales; by 1551, the official value of the cocoa bean was 140 to the real.

Cobs, crude pieces minted by the Spaniards, were the first coins in the Western Hemisphere. They were sliced from silver bars, then struck with hand dies.

What does the term "Cob" mean used in relation to early Real pieces?

The term refers to a crude type of Spanish dollar coined at Mexico City from the reign of Philip II until the middle of the reign of Philip V, and for a longer time at the Potosi Mint in Peru. The cob was hastily coined by hand-stamping slices of crude, irregularly rolled silver bars with crudely prepared dies, but with no sacrifice of weight and fineness. The word "Cob" is a corruption of the Spanish "Cabo de barra," meaning literally "end of the bar."

What is a "Piece of Eight"?

The term "piece of eight" is an unofficial name give to the Spanish piece of eight reales by the Brotherhood of Buccaneers. The coin was not itself a monetary unit but a multiple of the Spanish monetary unit, the real. The real was the equivalent of 12½ U.S. cents.

Storied piece of eight, or Spanish milled dollar, had decorative edge to prevent clipping. Fractional parts, or "bits," gave birth to the term still in use.

What is a "doubloon"?

The doubloon was a gold coin of Spain and Spanish America, first struck during the 14th century. Originally it was equal in value to eight gold escudos or 16 silver pesos. When Spain adopted the metric system in 1849, the doubloon was made equal to ten escudos or 100 reales, about the equivalent of five dollars.

What is a Pillar Dollar and what is a Milled Dollar?

The pillar dollar and the milled dollar were created simultaneously in the same coin in 1732 when the standard of the Spanish dollar was slightly lowered, the old design replaced with the imaginative Dos Mundos (Two Worlds) design, and the edge protected for the first time against clipping and shaving by a milling of floral design.

The design of two conjoined hemispheres resting upon the sea between two pillars and capped with the crown of Spain is symbolic of the Age of Exploration and the ambition of Spain. The conjoined worlds beneath the Spanish Crown symbolize the unity of hemispheres under the rule of Spain. The waves and the Pillars of Hercules symbolize that the western sea, rather than being the end of the world, is the gateway to new worlds. The amended motto, "Plus Ultra," on the pillars attests that, contrary to the warning of Hercules, there is "More Beyond" the Straits of Gibraltar.

The pillar dollar is the most famous crown of the Western Hemisphere, and belongs in the cabinet of every collector of America's coinage.

Was the Spanish-American piece of eight reales ever used in the United States for money?

The coins of Spain, minted in Mexico, served as the principal medium of exchange in the American colonies prior to the Revolution and the subsequent establishing of the U.S. Mint. They continued to circulate con-currently with U.S. coinage and as official legal tender until 1857.

What is a "Bit" piece?

"Bit" was a popular expression for the Spanish and Mexican silver 1-real piece. The value of a real or bit, 12½¢ U.S., was derived from the real being one eighth the value of a piece of eight reales, which was equal in value to the U.S. silver dollar. Logically, two reales or two bits were the equal of a U.S. quarter dollar, and four bits of a half dollar. The practice of calling a quarter "two bits" has survived to our time.

A persistent shortage of small change gave rise to the practice of cutting a piece of eight reales into appropriate half-moon and pie-shaped bit pieces which passed freely as minor coinage.

Can Mexico's history be traced through its coinage?

The thread of history is woven through the coinage of all nations.

Mexican coins relate the tales of feeble-minded monarchs, rabid revolutionaries, fighting priests, forceful reactionaries, an Austrian pretender, bandit presidents, and the birth and development of a republic.

They tell of a city founded on two marshy islands where an eagle devoured a snake; of a Great Temple erected atop a pyramid and sanctified with the

blood of 20,000 captives; of a warrior-priest society sufficiently advanced to devise calendars, irrigate crops and build walled cities - and primitive enough to cut the beating hearts from children to forestall calamities foretold by the entrails of goats.

They tell of the coming of the Great White God from across the seas, and of how he preached salvation through faith while he looted and enslaved; of a cruel and sanguinary struggle against the tyranny of foreign despot and native adventurer; of the triumph of humanism over reaction and the emergence of democracy's light from the dark night of suppression and indignity.

But in all they tell, they but again relate the theme of all men in all ages: the ceaseless struggle between superstition and intelligence, and between aspiration and the intransigeance of power.

I thought Mexico's peso was a silver coin, but I have one dated 1972 which appears to be struck of a nickel alloy. What's the story?

Mexico's is one of history's more storied silver coins. Its origins are tied to the rich heritage of the Spanish colonial eight reales coin which achieved such widespread international respect and was produced in great numbers at the mints of colonial Mexico. The coin's fine silver content was .9027 until 1918 when the fineness was debased to .800 and the total weight of the coin reduced by more than 30-percent. The fineness declined again in 1920, this time to .720, at which time the weight was reduced from 18.125 grams to 16.66 grams.

The peso remained a stable coin for the next 25 years, but in 1947 the standard was again reduced, this time to a .500 fineness and 14 gram weight. That lasted until 1950 when the standards became .300 fine and 13.333 grams for a single year coin issue. Coinage was resumed in 1957 with the weight raised to 16 grams, but the fineness debased to .100, at which it remained until the last silver pesos were struck in 1967. The peso was reintroduced as a nine gram copper-nickel coin in 1970.

How many mints have there been in Mexico?

The exact number is still debated. Including Crown and Revolutionary mints, there were probably no less than 23. The first and principal mint was at Mexico City. Other well-know mints were located at Chihuaha, Guadalajara, Guanajuato, Sombrerete, Zacatecas, Durango, Oaxaca and Valladolid.

When did Mexico first use paper money?

Mexico issued paper money for the first time in 1822, during the First Empire of Augustin I (Iturbide). The issue took the form of 1, 2 and 10 pesos promissory notes, printed uniface, and redeemable a year from issuance. General disapproval of the notes discredited the government and contributed to the downfall of Iturbide. The notes were demonetized on April 11, 1823, and their use authorized for part payment of taxes. Curiously, on May 12, 1823, a series of one-peso notes was authorized to redeem the unwanted first issue notes. They were printed on the blank backs of Papal Bulls of Indulgence, for which reason they are generally known as "Bull Notes."

Under how many monarchs did Mexico mint coins?

Coins were struck at mints located in Mexico during the reigns of eleven Spanish monarchs: Charles I (and Johanna), Philip II, Philip III, Philip IV, Charles II, Philip V, Louis I, Ferdinand VI, Charles III and Ferdinand VII. To these may be added the usurpers Iturbide (Augustin I) and Maximilian.

What is the monetary unit used in Mexico today?

The peso, which is divided into 100 centavos, and has depreciated to a value of less than one-half cent U.S. "Peso" is Spanish for "weight," or "unit of weight."

Did the "piece of-eight" have other names?

Many of them. They include Spanish dollar, milled dollar, pillar dollar, piastre, peso, 'dobe dollar and cob.

I have a number of different Mexican pesos featuring the patriot-priest Morelos. In each instance he is presented with his head wrapped in a cloth. Why is he depicted in this unusual manner?

The coins you mention are an unusual example of realistic, rather than idealistic, coin portraiture. Morelos suffered continuously from severe headaches, the pain of which he sought to relieve by tightly binding his head with a kerchief.

What is meant by the terms "Maximiliano," "Balanza," and "Caballito"?

They are names given by Mexicans to various types of their peso. "Maximiliano" refers to the 1866-67 peso issued by Emperor Maximilian; "Balanza" to the 1869-73 peso with design of balance scales; "Caballito" to the 1910-14 peso featuring Liberty on a horse.

I am confused by the identity of the king who ruled Spain (and Mexico) from 1516 to 1556. Some call him Charles I, and others Charles V. Which is correct?

Both. Johanna, the third child of Ferdinand and Isabella, succeeded to the Spanish throne upon the death of Ferdinand in 1516, but because she was mentally incompetent, her son Charles was appointed to rule in her name. Charles ruled as both Charles I, king of Spain, and Charles V, Holy Roman emperor.

How many different mint marks were used by the mint at Mexico City?

The mark most frequently utilized by the mint at Mexico City consists of the small letter "o" over the capital letter "M," but instances are known where it appears as M, Mo, *M•X*, and the letters Mxo in a vertical arrangement of small "o" above medium "x" above large "M." Mxo appears exclusively on gold coins issued from approximately 1681 to 1713. The mark *M•X* was used on all denominations of silver in 1733.

When did Mexico issue a coin in the unusual denomination of "1 Onza"?

It didn't. The 1 Onza is a silver bullion piece containing 1 troy ounce (480 grains) of .925 fine silver. It was issued in 1949 to help dispose of a large amount of silver bullion, and to demonstrate the exceptional quality of the work of the Mexico Mint in hopes of enticing orders for the minting of foreign coinage. Collectors include the 1 Onza in collections of Mexican coinage or world crowns because it is crown size, and because its design depicts the coinage themes of screw press and balance scales.

I recently saw a Mexican peso which bore the unusual motto "Muera Huerta," which in loose translation wills or wishes the death of Huerta, one of the prominent figures of the Mexican Revolution of 1910-1917. Can you tell me the origin of this coin?

The 1910-1917 Revolution was a time of unparalleled violence and confusion. The various guerrilla leaders - Villa, Zapata, Carranza, Obregon - fought each other even as they struggled to unseat Huerta, who had seized control of the Mexican government, and install his successor. Pancho Villa in particular hated Huerta intensely for causing the death of Madero, the mild intellectual who started the modern revolution, and for his own close brush with death at the hands of Huerta's firing squad. To publicize his hatred, he caused a silver peso to be struck in 1914 at Cuencame, Durango, on which was inscribed the motto MUERA HUERTA, or "Death to Huerta." Huerta was so incensed by the existence of Villa's "Death Wish" peso that he ordered the immediate execution of anyone found with the coin in his possession.

Foreign Coins

I have a silver-dollar-sized coin that portrays a queen on the obverse and a double-headed eagle with shield on the reverse. It is dated 1780, but it looks brand new. Is this a real coin?

You have the Queen of Current Coins, the Fat Lady of Numismatics, the dollar that is not a dollar. You have the renowned Maria Theresa thaler of Austria, which is not a thaler, but a bullion disc of 26.0668 grams of .833 fine silver, and is neither legal tender in its homeland nor bears a mark of value. You have an unofficial trade dollar that has been minted since 1780, and is still struck with the original date. You do not have a valuable coin, but you do have one of the most romantic issues in the lore of coindom.

This coin is the favorite trade dollar of traders and tribesmen in the coastal areas of the Red Sea and Persian Gulf because of its constant standard, unchanging design, and its intricate engraving and edge, which make it difficult to counterfeit and impossible to shave.

What is a "cartwheel," as the term is applied to foreign coins?

During the eighteenth century, the obsolete equipment of the Royal Mint proved to be incapable of supplying the expanded coinage requirement of England. The coinage of copper was neglected to produce gold and silver coins. By the late 1700s, the only copper coins in circulation were regal coins worn smooth, underweight counterfeits, and a hodgepodge of private tokens issued by exasperated merchants in facilitating business transactions.

Finally in 1797 England issued a pence and twopence of sufficient weight to discourage counterfeiting. The penny contained an ounce of copper, and the twopenny, which was as large as our silver dollar and twice as thick, contained two ounces. They were promptly dubbed "cartwheels" because of their tremendous size, and because they were made with a broad, flat rim on which the legend was incused.

These were the first English regal coins to be made with steam power.

The term "cartwheel" is also sometimes applied to U.S. silver dollars issued in the late 1800s and early 1900s, and similar sized silver coins of other countries.

I have a United States silver dollar dated 1875 and on the back it says "Trade Dollar." There are a number of marks which resemble Chinese characters on the coin. Could you explain this?

The United States trade dollar was introduced in 1873 to complete with the Mexican trade dollar which had obtained popularity with Oriental merchants.

The Chinese merchant was a suspicious fellow who examined each coin closely to determine its genuineness. Certain merchants who commanded the respect of their fellows stamped their "chop mark" on authenticated coins to inform others that they were genuine. Some dollars so treated are so covered with chop marks as to be bent and nearly unrecognizable. Others with four or five neatly executed and spaced marks are prized by some collectors.

Did the United States ever issue colonial coins of its own?

The United States Philippine coinage might be so considered. After liberating the Philippine Islands from Spanish dominion, the United States issued a regular coinage for the islands. It commenced in 1903 and continued until 1945.

The obverse bore the legend "United States of America," and the reverse bore, in addition to the design, the denomination in Spanish and the name "Filipinas." The coinage was issued in 1/2, 1, 5, 10, 20, and 50 centavos and a silver 1 peso.

Can I exchange foreign coins for U.S. money?

The machinery for so doing is available in the foreign exchange departments of some commercial banks in the larger cities. However, in view of the fluctuating rate of exchange, the low value of most foreign coins, the commission charged for the exchange, and the fact that many issues of older foreign coinage have been devalued, the transaction is of dubious worth unless you have a great deal of foreign money to exchange.

Did Hawaii ever issue its own coins?

Prior to becoming a territory of the United States, the independent Kingdom of Hawaii issued a modest number and variety of coins. The first official coins were the copper cents of 1847. These bore on obverse the facing bust of King Kamehameha III, and on reverse the denomination "Hapa Haneri," meaning "one hundreth part."

Apart from some pattern coins, the next issue was struck in 1883 and consisted of a silver dime, quarter dollar, half dollar and dollar. The obverse bore

the head of King Kalakaua I to right. Additional patterns struck in the 1890s complete the coinage of the Kingdom of Hawaii. All of the coins are scarce, and command substantial premiums on the coin market.

I have seen a number of coins which carry a portrait of a King of England on the obverse along with legends which attest to his being King of England. However, on the reverse is carried the name of some other countries, such as South Africa, West Africa, East Africa, etc. What is the reason for this?

At the height of colonialism prior to World War I, the British Empire embraced a fourth of the habitable land area of the globe and influenced the happiness of a fifth of its people. The colonies which were permitted their own coinage acknowledged British sovereignty by depicting the British monarch on the obverse of their coins. At this time it was said that 80 percent of the coins in the pocket of an American sailor home from the sea had been minted under British auspices.

The surge of nationalism born between two wars lowered the union jack upon dune and headland, and brought independence to most of the former British colonies. Those which chose independence within the British Commonwealth have, in most instances, continued the tradition of a monarchic coinage.

Does the portrait of Edward VIII, the king who gave up a throne for love, appear on the coins of England or the colonies?

No English or colonial coins bearing a portrait of Edward VIII were released for circulation. The Royal Mint struck a few complete sets of Edward VIII coinage for English institutions. Possibly twelve of the 12 sided, brass threepence pieces were released to vending machine companies for testing purposes. Most were returned, but a few are in private collections. The Royal Mint classifies them as patterns.

Colonial coins bearing the name of Edward VIII, but not his portrait, were released by East Africa, West Africa, New Guinea, Fiji, and the Indian states of Kutch and Jodhpur.

I have what appears to be an English copper halfpenny, dated 1793, which bears the portrait of Sir Isaac Newton. However, I can't find it listed among English coins of that period. What do I have?

You have an English eighteenth-century trade token of the type issued by merchants of England, Scotland, Ireland and Wales from 1787 to 1804. They are generally called Conder tokens, in recognition of James Conder, who compiled the first comprehensive catalog of the series in 1798. These tokens were issued by private sources to alleviate an annoying shortage of regal copper coins. It is estimated that the series contains approximately 10,000 historically attuned tokens, including counterfeits, mules, and varieties of date, die and edge.

What is the largest official silver coin in circulation?

It's a giant 1975-dated 20-pa'anga coin from the Pacific Kingdom of Tonga. The piece measures 62 millimeters (almost 2½ inches) in diameter and weighs 140 grams. The previous title holder was Panama's 1971 silver 20-Balboas, measuring in at 61 millimeters, with 2,000 grains of .925 silver. Both coins were issued for circulation, but the extent of commercial use is questionable. In 1985 a limited issue 25 pounds coin commemorative of the Falkland Islands' "self sufficiency," with a diameter of 65mm and silver weight of 4.82 ounces sterling (2,313.6 grains), technically supplanted the Tonga coin as the world's heaviest silver coin. This offering has been supplanted by Communist China's 1986 dated 50 Yuan coin commemorating the 120th anniversary of the birth of Dr. Sun Yat-Sen, a 70mm diameter issue struck of .999 fine silver and weighing five ounces (155.52 grams).

In recent years I have seen more and more advertised coins designated as "NCLTs". What are they?

Coins designated non-circulating legal tender (NCLT) are those created and marketed under the agencies of sovereign governments expressly for sale to collectors. They are primarily individual coins of a commemorative nature which invariably are sold at prices substantially in excess of their face values, and often do not have a counterpart in the same or a base metal which were released to circulation. Officially they are legal tender, and can be employed as such, but they are not intended to serve as a medium of exchange.

Is it really a fact that English pennies were once made of gold?

The deeper one delves into the science of numismatics, the more he comes to realize that money isn't what it used to be. The now lowly penny was the principal coin of the Middle Ages, and in England was made of silver until a change to copper was made in 1797. In the 12th century, a silver English penny would pay the rent of a cottage for a year. In 1257, Henry III caused gold pennies to be struck to represent the value of 20 silver pennies.

I have been told that when Matthew Boulton produced the massive 1797 "Cartwheel" coinage for England, he intended that in addition to their utility as coins, they be used for gauging weights and measures. Can you explain how this worked?

Matthew Boulton can explain it better: "I intend there shall be a coincidence between our Money, Weight and Measures, by making 8 twopenny pieces 1 lb, and to measure 1 foot; 16 penny pieces 1 lb and 17 to measure 2 feet; 32 half-pence 1 lb, and 10 to measure 1 foot."

I recently picked up a brass piece dated 1837 that appears to be English. It has a young Victoria head on the obverse and a horseman and multiheaded dragon on reverse. The legend reads, "To Hanover." Is this a 19th century British token?

Although the "To Hanover" pieces may have seen limited service as tokens, they are generally considered to be game counters inspired by an incident in British history. Hanover, a small independent kingdom in Germany, was from 1714 to 1837 ruled by the same sovereign as Great Britain. Victoria became Queen of Great Britain in 1837 upon the death of William IV. She did not, however, become Queen of Hanover. By the law of Hanover, a woman could not ascend the throne. Accordingly, Ernest Augustus, duke of Cumberland, fifth son of George III, was appointed sovereign and took up residence in Hanover. Hence the legend, "To Hanover."

Were the British "Model Coins" that resemble the 1792 U.S. silver-center cents of Henry Voight intended to be patterns for a copper coinage of convenient size but good intrinsic value?

Joseph Moore may have had something like that in mind when he privately made the so-called "Model Coins," although the center plug, made in imitation of a genuine British coin, is white-metal, not silver. Moore issued his "Model Coins" (the name refers to the word MODEL that appears on them) in great quantities, in denominations of 1/2, 1/4, 1/8, 1/16 and 1/32 of a farthing. Whatever the pieces were intended to be, they proved to be so popular with the people that the Royal Mint had to publicly disown them as official issues.

Numismatic Investment

Is it true that you can buy proof sets each year and be assured of a profit?

You can buy proof sets each year - from the Mint if you order promptly and from dealers thereafter - and in most years when proof sets have been issued (1936-1942, 1950-1964, 1968 to present), these sets have appreciated in value at the year's end.

However, when coins are consigned to the marketplace they become simple commodities or articles of commerce, and as such are subject to the same laws that govern the economic performance of pork bellies or peanuts. Values have risen and fallen in response to supply and demand. The 1957 proof set depreciated to the point where some collectors sold them for less than their initial cost before they recovered to a satisfactory level. The 1964 Kennedy proof set rode a wave of nostalgia to a high of $16, then tumbled to a value of about $5 in 1977, before recovering to earlier levels. In recent years, the profit performance of proof sets has lagged behind that of commemoratives, type coins and gold but there is little reason to suppose that they will not again increase in popularity. It is, however, unrealistic to suppose that any of the high mintage sets of recent years will parallel the performance of the 1936 set, which has a 1985 value in excess of $4,000.

What makes rolls of coins worth more than their face value?

Hope. A calculated guess based on the experience of prior time.

If you check a price list of uncirculated Lincoln cents (to cite but one example), you will notice that the pre-1934 coins are considerably higher priced than those that follow. The short supply of pre-1934 uncirculated cents revealed by their higher prices was created when the rolls of the teens and twenties that collectors had squirreled away were taken from cigar box and trunk during the early hardship years of the Great Depression and given to the butcher, who fed them into circulation.

The erosion of supply wasn't fully appreciated until the hobby entered an expansionary phase following World War II. Then collectors, sadly realizing the extent of the profit that had gone awry, began hoarding rolls and turning a handsome profit on them within an acceptable time. Their success attracted the speculators, and in the early 1960s the roll market boomed with an artificial prosperity created by speculators selling their rolls to each other. Inevitably, the bubble burst, with a lot of them "taking a bath."

Intelligent roll collecting is essential to the future growth of the hobby. But it should be remembered that the rolls must ultimately be broken up and sold to collectors as individual coins in a marketplace where the laws of supply and demand remain operative. A quantity release at any one time can only depress their value.

Is collecting any type of coin a good investment?

No!

The hobby collector - be it of coins, back-scratchers or Bavarian beer mugs - is occasionally persuaded to a purchase by impulse or sentiment. Indulging infrequent lapses into irrationality is part of the fun of maintaining a hobby. But the strictly investment collector cannot afford to indulge impulse or sentiment. His purchases must be informed and selective. He must avoid historically rewarding but neglected types, slow movers, common dates and low grades. He must regard his collection not as an end, but as the means to an end outside the hobby.

Is it really true that I can put my children through school with the profits from investing in coins?

It is true that large profits have been made through judicious coin investments, and it is highly probable that such profits have been sufficient to provide a college education for the investor's children, primarily over the past thirty years.

Realistically, there is a risk inherent in any investment and there can be no real assurance that your coin investments will create the necessary income to provide a college education for your children.

Are coins a good investment? Can they go down in price?

Coins can be a good investment. And they can go down in price.

A phenomenon of coin investment is that the casual collector who wouldn't think of buying a stock without consulting a broker, will plunge into coin investment with the random restraint of a bull in a china shop. Approach coin investment with the same research and intelligent concern you would bring to investment in real estate, stocks and bonds or commodity futures.

Could I buy any new coin, hold it for a few years and make money on it?

Not necessarily. Time is the essential ingredient, and "a few years" might not be enough of it. It is true that collectors prefer uncirculated specimens, and that even collectors of modest means are not reluctant to pay a small premium to upgrade the appearance of their collection and its long-run potential for appreciation. It is also true that in most instances uncirculated coins properly stored to prevent tarnish and discoloration, and kept a sufficient number of years, appreciate in value, sometimes spectacularly.

Still, the indiscriminate buying of new coins for investment should not be recommended. It should be remembered that even a profit can mean losing money if the capital could have been more profitably employed in selective coin investment.

Are freak "mint errors" a good investment?

A number of specific major mint errors - 1922 plain or filled-die cent, 1955 double die obverse cent, 1937-D 3-legged buffalo nickel, a number of overdates - are established as desired and valuable coins. Several examples of off-center strikes, and coins struck on planchets of incorrect size or metal also command impressive premiums.

Mint errors - die breaks, blobs, multiple mint marks, laminations, rotated dies, etc. - have no widely accepted fixed price, and are worth what someone is willing to pay for them. However, the rapid growth in the number of mint-error enthusiasts could well invoke the laws of supply and demand at some future date.

Can anybody make money on coins?

Only in the sense that anyone can become president: the opportunity is available to all. Certainly money has been made on the coins. It has also been lost. Almost invariably, the one who makes money buying and selling coins is also one who is well grounded in the fundamentals of the hobby. Compulsive gambling is not investment.

Is there any course available which would teach me the "know how" of the hobby of coin collecting?

Not in the academic sense - but neither is there a school to train presidents. Desire is the motive and application is the means to acquiring a working knowledge of coin collecting. There are, of course, valuable aids to a thoughtful program of self-application. The better-run coin clubs include lectures and panel discussions in their activities. Authoritative books on every phase and field of the hobby are readily available from coin shops, mail-order dealers and, frequently, public libraries. Subscribe to one or more of the national coin publications. They will keep you informed of the references currently available, and through their book reviews acquaint you with the theme of the latest offerings as they become available. Build your library as you build your collection. "Growth through knowledge" is more than a catch phrase.

It seems to me that this hobby of coin collecting is based entirely on dollars and cents. Is this correct?

If your premise were correct, there would be no collector interest in Conder tokens, which have appreciated but slightly in value over the past 175 years; nor an expanding interest in transportation tokens, minor mint errors, wooden nickels, etc. The hobby collector, one who builds a collection chiefly for the pleasure, relaxation and increased knowledge it affords him, is the kingpin of the hobby. Without him, the dealers, coin press and numismatic speculators could not exist for an hour. The collector came first; the others followed to service his need.

What type of coins are best to buy for investment?

Supply and demand are the dominant persuasions of the marketplace. In the world of coins, demand is expressed in two ways. First, the demand of type; there is a greater demand for the common Lincoln cent than for scarce Byzantine bronze. Within the desired type, the demand is greatest for the coins of higher grade and lower mintage. Supply is meaningless unless there is a demand for the type - an 800-year-old denier of Richard the Lion Hearted can be purchased for under $10. Over the years, the highest grades of the lowest mintage coins within a demand type have proven to be the soundest investment.

Can you offer a short-cut method of making a quick profit in coins?

If we could, we wouldn't be selling books. An honest quick profit is more often the result of a fortunate coincidence of judgment and timing.

Are gold coins a good investment?

Gold coins contain a dual investment potential, one derived from their value as collector items and the other from their intrinsic bullion value.

Gold coins on the numismatic market have exhibited a modest but determined rate of value increase. It has been calculated that if a collector had obtained one each of the double eagles ($20 gold piece) by year and mint mark (exclusive of the 1927D) from 1908 to 1932, and held them until 1987, his collection would have cost him $920, and would have been worth $172,710. This is equal to an annual compound interest return of 7.85 percent.

The double eagle contains slightly less than an ounce of gold. Based on the present official U.S. price of gold ($42.44 per ounce), each coin contains $40.85 worth of the metal. Now that the gold-reserve requirements for Eed-

eral Reserve notes and deposits have been abolished, both the monetary role and official price of gold are symbolic.

The age-old lure of gold should insure the continuing popularity of gold coins as collector items. Their future as bullion has yet to be decided.

I have several old large-size paper notes with consecutive numbers. Are they a good investment?

Paper money in general is not considered to have the investment potential of coins. Collector enthusiasm is discouraged by the higher face values of paper money. However, there is a definite market in paper money, and a consequent potential for the emergence of "blue chips." In regard to the serial numbers, each paper note is unique in that it has a serial number that is not duplicated elsewhere in the series. Consequently, the serial number in itself is not usually significant.

What effect has the withdrawing and melting of silver coins by the government had on their individual value and investment potential?

The Federal Reserve's three-year attempt to cull the nation's silver coinage and melt it for industrial use was less than 20 percent successful, leaving something in excess of $1,784,120,000 worth of silver coinage minted subsequent to 1940 in the hands of dealers, collectors, numismatic investors and bullion speculators. A substantial portion of this private holding has already been melted, and more will be. The ultimate effect of the hoarding and melting upon the value of individual silver coins cannot be determined at this time.

Certainly, mintage figures are now a questionable indicator of a silver coin's rarity. It isn't unlikely that some of the silver coins now considered to be relative rarities will, in years to come, prove to be more plentiful than some of the high-mintage issues that were consigned to the melting pot.

At what point does the bullion value of U.S. silver coins surpass their face value?

The monetary value of silver was $1.2929 per ounce. At the time the market value of silver bullion hit that level, the value of the precious metal contained in a regular issue dime, quarter, half or dollar minted from 1873 through 1964 matched the coin's face value. In the case of silver wartime nickels, the break point was a bullion market value of approximately 90 cents. The following chart shows the relationship between the bullion value of U.S. silver coins and incremental bullion market levels, including .400 fine silver halves (1965-70) and dollars (1971-70). This chart also presents values for the bullion contents of Canadian silver coins minted from 1920 through 1968.

Silver Price Per Ounce	$5.25	$5.50	$5.75	$6.00	$6.25	$6.50	$6.75	$7.00	$7.25	$7.50
U.S. 5¢ .350 Fine (Wartime)	.30	.31	.33	.34	.35	.37	.38	.39	.41	.42
U.S. 50¢ .400 Fine (1965-70)	.78	.81	.85	.89	.93	.96	1.00	1.04	1.07	1.11
U.S. $1.00 .400 Fine (1971-76)	1.66	1.74	1.82	1.90	1.98	2.06	2.14	2.21	2.29	2.37
U.S. 10¢ .900 Fine (Pre-1965)	.38	.40	.42	.43	.45	.47	.49	.51	.52	.54
U.S. 25¢ .900 Fine (Pre-1965)	.95	.99	1.04	1.08	1.13	1.18	1.22	1.27	1.31	1.36
U.S. 50¢ .900 Fine (Pre-1965)	1.90	1.99	2.08	2.17	2.26	2.35	2.44	2.53	2.62	2.71
U.S. $1.00 .900 Fine (To 1935)	4.06	4.25	4.45	4.64	4.84	5.03	5.22	5.41	5.61	5.80
Canada 10¢ .800 Fine (1920-67)	.32	.33	.35	.36	.38	.39	.41	.42	.44	.45
Canada 25¢ .800 Fine (1920-67)	.79	.83	.87	.90	.94	.98	1.02	1.05	1.09	1.13
Canada 50¢ .800 Fine (1920-67)	1.58	1.65	1.75	1.80	1.88	1.95	2.03	2.10	2.18	2.25
Canada $1 .800 Flne (1936-67)	3.15	3.30	3.45	3.60	3.75	3.90	4.05	4.20	4.35	4.50
Canada 10¢ .500 Fine (1967-68)	.20	.21	.22	.23	.24	.24	.26	.26	.27	.28
Canada 25¢ .500 Fine (1967-68)	.50	.52	.54	.56	.59	.61	.64	.66	.68	.70

Silver Price Per Ounce	$7.75	$8.00	$8.25	$8.50	$8.75	$9.00	$9.25	$9.50	$9.75	$10.00
U.S. 5¢ .350 Fine (Wartime)	.44	.45	.46	.48	.49	.51	.52	.53	.55	.56
U.S. 50¢ .400 Fine (1965-70)	1.15	1.18	1.22	1.26	1.29	1.33	1.37	1.40	1.44	1.48
U.S. $1.00 .400 Fine (1971-76)	2.45	2.53	2.61	2.69	2.77	2.85	2.93	3.00	3.08	3.16
U.S. 10¢ .900 Fine (Pre-1965)	.56	.58	.60	.61	.63	.65	.67	.69	.71	.72
U.S. 25¢ .900 Fine (Pre-1965)	1.40	1.45	1.49	1.54	1.58	1.63	1.67	1.72	1.76	1.81
U.S. 50¢ .900 Fine (Pre-1965)	2.80	2.89	2.98	3.07	3.16	3.26	3.34	3.44	3.53	3.61
U.S. $1.00 .900 Fine (To 1935)	5.99	6.19	6.38	6.57	6.77	6.96	7.15	7.35	7.54	7.73
Canada 10¢ .800 Fine (1920-67)	.47	.48	.50	.51	.53	.54	.56	.57	.59	.60
Canada 25¢ .800 Fine (1920-67)	1.16	1.20	1.24	1.28	1.31	1.35	1.39	1.43	1.46	1.50
Canada 50¢ .800 Fine (1920-67)	2.33	2.40	2.48	2.55	2.63	2.70	2.78	2.85	2.93	3.00
Canada $1 .800 Fine (1935-67)	4.65	4.80	4.95	5.10	5.25	5.40	5.55	5.70	5.85	6.00
Canada 10¢ .500 Fine (1967-68)	.29	.30	.31	.32	.33	.34	.35	.36	.37	.38
Canada 25¢ .500 Fine (1967-68)	.73	.75	.77	.80	.82	.84	.87	.89	91	.94

Key Word Index

— E —

— F —

— G —

— H —

— I —

— J —

— K —

— L —

— M —